LEARNING AND DEVELOPMENT

HR FUNDAMENTALS

LEARNING AND DEVELOPMENT

Rebecca
Page-Tickell

KoganPage

LONDON PHILADELPHIA NEW DELHI

Publisher's note

Every possible effort has been made to ensure that the information contained in this book is accurate at the time of going to press, and the publishers and author cannot accept responsibility for any errors or omissions, however caused. No responsibility for loss or damage occasioned to any person acting, or refraining from action, as a result of the material in this publication can be accepted by the editor, the publishers or the author.

First published in Great Britain and the United States in 2014 by Kogan Page Limited

2nd Floor, 45 Gee Street	1518 Walnut Street, Suite 1100	4737/23 Ansari Road
London EC1V 3RS	Philadelphia PA 19102	Daryaganj
United Kingdom	USA	New Delhi 110002
www.koganpage.com		India

© Rebecca Page-Tickell, 2014

ISBN   978 0 7494 6988 7
E-ISBN   978 0 7494 6989 4

British Library Cataloguing-in-Publication Data

A CIP record for this book is available from the British Library.

Library of Congress Cataloging-in-Publication Data

Page-Tickell, Rebecca.
    Learning and development / Rebecca Page-Tickell. – 1st Edition.
        pages cm. – (HR fundamentals)
        ISBN 978-0-7494-6988-7 (paperback) – ISBN 978-0-7494-6989-4 (ebk)
    1. Organizational learning.   2. Personnel management.   3. Employees–Training of.   I. Title.
        HD58.82.P34 2014
        658.3′124–dc23
                                                                            2014014540

Typeset by Graphicraft Limited, Hong Kong
Printed and bound by CPI Group (UK) Ltd, Croydon, CR0 4YY

CONTENTS

LIST OF FIGURES

LIST OF TABLES

PART ONE

FUNDAMENTALS OF LEARNING AND DEVELOPMENT

Defining learning and development

Introduction

In this book, I will address learning and development in the workplace. Learning and development (L&D) is the process used by both owners and employees in a business/organization to endow it with all the people capabilities and resources required for its ongoing success. It primarily involves the acquisition of knowledge, skills and attitudes by both groups and individuals. It consists of a range of tools and techniques, typically combined into a programme following an overarching goal and philosophy linked to strategic business goals. This is typically coordinated through an organization to support the achievement of overarching strategic goals, at organizational, team and individual levels. In this way, a learning and development strategy is built to serve the current and emerging needs of the organization to build sustainable success.

In this chapter I will develop this definition further to uncover some of the fundamental principles of learning and development. Later on in the book I will discuss how to design and deliver effective learning and development. I will take account of the various stakeholders involved and identify what makes an effective learning and development intervention as well as how to identify its effectiveness.

The definition of learning and development above indicates that the focus is primarily on the outcome of enhancing people and organizational capability. It may be inferred from this that it involves a smorgasbord of perspectives and approaches for and from varying individuals and groups. Like motherhood and apple pie it is typically considered 'a good thing'. However,

FIGURE 1.1   Primary factors impacting on learning and development

closer analysis reveals that this multiple perspective and influence can limit its effectiveness. As anyone who has sought to deliver learning and development will attest, the conflicting requirements of each group, approach and perspective rapidly muddy the waters.

Figure 1.1 aims to represent some of the core factors impacting on successful delivery of learning and development. The book will expand upon this multiplicity of demands to enable the practitioner to identify a successful approach in their own context.

I will also discuss the various constraints and influencing factors on the learning and development function itself. I will address a range of approaches to structuring the function, from embedding it within strategic business units, through to outsourcing it to external organizations, almost in its entirety. This review of the place and importance of the function is important in view of its place in the organization and the impact it can have on elements such as employee engagement and organizational commitment. I discuss issues around responsibility for learning, the history of training and development and also how the outcomes of learning and development can impact on an organization's capabilities. The approach is not entirely uncritical and I will question the value that learning could add and seek to understand why it is not always leveraged to its fullest extent.

I will also view learning and development through the eyes of the organization. How does learning and development contribute to organizational capability and strategic development? In short, how does it help the organization gain and retain a competitive advantage?

Finally, I will touch on some of the new developments in this area and I will consider a case study that demonstrates both the benefits and complexities associated with learning and development.

What is 'learning and development'?

We are all involved in a constant, ongoing process of learning and development. It happens consistently in our homes, during our leisure time and in our workplace as well. It is said that as humans we either change or die! Well, the process of learning and development is changing, adapting and growing to meet and overcome challenges and change. Every stage of life involves change and we could profit from reviewing how we have adapted to some of the major changes in our own lives. How did we predict the change? To what did we attribute it? One of the fathers of psychology, William James (1890) noted: 'Whilst part of what we perceive comes through our senses from the object before us, another part (and it may be the larger part) always comes out of our own mind.' That is, we do not perceive reality directly, rather we mediate it through our expectations and experiences. So, if we have benefited from a learning intervention such as coaching in the past we will approach it with a far more positive frame of mind than someone who undertook coaching reluctantly as part of a redundancy package.

This process of attribution impacts how I understand what is happening around us and how I engage with it. It also impacts the choices that I make, for example: What resources have I had access to and have I gathered to overcome the challenge? I probably had some prior experience that I could adapt to the new experience. Consider that the first day in your first job is not a million miles from the first day in your most recent job. You probably discussed it in advance with friends or a partner or other supporter and whilst you were travelling this change you probably reviewed what was happening and what it meant with those same people. Then, once the change had become established and predictable you could look forward to the next developments.

In our home life this may be focused on personal relationships, a move across the country or having children. In the workplace it may be a change of market conditions, a new manager, a new role within an organization or redundancy. Each of these are changes for an individual to predict, meet and deal with.

The same process applies to an organization, however, the added layer of complexity is that the number of attributions and perspectives is roughly equal to the number of employees. Therefore, there is a clear need for organizational management of the process of learning and development, focusing on the learning from each situation to draw out and share the learning points. This enables a more focused and coordinated response across the organization to the change.

It is important to note that I am discussing learning as opposed to training. This term is now something of a relic, evoking as it does a bygone era of paternalistic organizations that 'knew' what their employees should be doing and provided all the tools to enable them to learn, with a final position of having 'learnt' everything that was required for that role.

The emphasis here is on the active learning on the part of the employee, with them taking responsibility for their learning in partnership with the employing organization. The organization may be one among a number of bodies who additionally collaborate with the employee, for example, professional bodies such as:

- Royal College of Nursing;
- Solicitors Regulation Authority;
- Institution of Mechanical Engineers.

It may also include voluntary organizations such as:

- Sea Cadets;
- Scouts;
- Rotary International.

The organization will ideally act as a resource guiding the individual employee as well as teams and various groups to develop in line with the organization's strategic aims. In this way the organizational capability can be built simultaneously with individual skills, knowledge and attitudes.

Today's world is fast-changing and unpredictable. What we knew as children is not what our children know now. Our expectations are dissimilar to their expectations. Who could have guessed that generations following the baby boomers would experience reduced standards of living? Until very recently this was completely unimaginable. Yet, it is the reality that we are slowly starting to face. This disconcerting fluidity in our environment is not entirely unrecognized, Alvin Toffler (1970) wrote about the rapidly increasing pace of change in his book, *Future Shock*. Whilst less-studied today, this book contains some important insights about how in this new 'information revolution', the levers for success revolve around adaptability and agility of thinking. Interviewed by *New Scientist* in 1994 he commented,

> I don't think you can understand today's changes without recognizing the revolutionary nature of these changes... I say we are going from a brute-force economy to a brain-force economy and it's clear that skills and knowledge are becoming the central resource for economic activity. If I had studied economics I would have been taught that the factors of production are land, labour and capital. 'Knowledge' doesn't appear. Today, knowledge not only must appear in that list, it dominates the others.

I would add that knowledge should be complemented by skills, and the capacity to learn how to change pace and direction through being alert to events around us. This is the very essence of learning – to be alert, adapt, adopt and attain:

- *Be alert* to the changing circumstances, know what is required of you now and what might be required in the future, both near and far.

- *Adapt* your expectations and goals to your current situation.

- *Adopt* the skills and attitudes required of you in your new situation.

- *Attain* the levels of performance required of you.

A critical approach to learning and development

I noted earlier that learning and development can be considered 'a good thing' in general. You will have seen from the definition that almost anything can be considered 'learning and development'. Indeed, in some situations such an iterative approach is no bad thing! Particularly in rapidly changing market conditions agility and the capacity to both adapt and respond rapidly to ambiguous and almost undecipherable market conditions is life-saving for the organization.

However, in more stable conditions the unstructured approach, which incorporates any and all activity, is more likely to damage the organization. This is because it tends to follow each manager's individual preferences and whims rather than building on a strategic intent to build capabilities and human resources. It can therefore leave the organization somewhat weakened with a spiky profile of excellence in certain areas with the attending weakness in other areas. Certainly, many years ago I experienced an organization-wide development activity that still leaves me wondering about its value or legitimacy. It was the early 90s, and working in the City of London, appearance was very important. As a result, employees across the whole organization were styled. Depending on your level you received anything from a couple of days' one-to-one clothes advice, to a group session. The one-to-one session involved bringing in a selection of clothes to discuss what colours and style suited, what image they projected and how to build a capsule wardrobe. This has all been useful advice for me personally and seeing senior engineers discussing how pale yellow and pink suited them is a fond memory that will stay with me! How it raised the capability of the organization however, is something I have struggled to understand for some time. Indeed, in today's terms of highly stretched resources, such expenditure seems nothing short of profligate.

The example above demonstrates that it is essential as a human resources (HR) practitioner to adopt a very critical approach to learning and development at all levels. After all, you and your organization are the ones who are going to have to live with the results! A consultancy may be able to come in and give a very smooth pitch, but is their product really everything it purports to be, and, importantly, what is the core issue you are seeking to address?

Organizational development through human resource development

An organization is, in many ways, simply an agreement between a group of people to share in an endeavour or enterprise. In its simplest form these people arrange themselves in a hierarchy, gather resources, manipulate those resources to add value and barter with others for money. Seen from its simplest perspective the organization has a limited range of resources, the raw materials, the transformation process and the trading. The people involved are at the heart of each of these stages. So, it follows that in order to improve any of these stages, the people themselves must be developed, perhaps in knowledge, skill, attitude, understanding, capacity to work together, innovate. This approach is at the root of the human capital model that is taught and followed by many of those who make decisions concerning organizational development. Essentially, this focuses on developing knowledge and skill in order to meet current, emerging and future challenges in a competitive marketplace.

Whilst the organization itself may have a clear plan of what it has agreed to do and where it wants to go, there are many other organizations fighting for the same ground and they may be faster, cheaper and higher quality. To compete effectively our organization must match and supersede them in any one of these areas. A clear way to do this is to develop the human element of the mix to improve all other elements. However, there is competition among organizations for ownership of resources, including human resources. It is therefore in the best interest of an organization to engage with its human resources to develop both them and its own capabilities, in order to develop a sustainable stream of talent to maintain market position over the longer term. Learning and development processes provide the skilled and able human resources that organizational development processes capitalize on for the long-term benefit of the organization.

Learning and development processes enable organizations to meet competitive challenges. There is a broad range of challenges that organizations may meet. However, there are two main categories to be considered; short, sharp, crisis-type situations and long-term, slow market shifts. Each of these requires different responses from those in charge of the organization to manage and navigate these challenges. Learning and development processes provide a way of developing those in the organization to be ready to meet these challenges. For example, through the use of workshops and learning intervention in observing market signals, senior managers may become skilled in spotting market trends. Occasionally, these may provide a major challenge to a core product and need addressing as a matter of urgency.

This approach can be seen in the example of organizations such as Google that use a range of strategies to develop intrapreneurs. These are individuals who have a spark of creativity and innovation and generate new product ideas. Different organizations adopt a range of approaches to either stifle or encourage these employees. Within Google, structural support is given by allowing employees to spend about a day a week working on projects of their own choosing. A good proportion of Google's innovative products come from this employee-led time. These interventions are at the cusp of learning and development and also knowledge management, and demonstrate how organizations need to take an aligned approach to ensure the ongoing development of both individual and organization to reap the rewards of competitive advantage.

I will be developing these ideas in later chapters where I address a range of approaches and tools that organizations may use to enable a sustainable competitive advantage through learning and development.

Emerging developments

A final area that I will address in this book is the development of new areas within learning and development. A number of these come from psychology and involve an enhanced understanding of how people tick and the extent to which the brain is 'plastic'. This suggests that the brain is even more complex than originally thought and that through millions of specific connections the brain is capable of adapting to new information and situations. This is mediated by our own experiences and understanding of ourselves. For example, the importance of mindsets in approaching a development opportunity. An individual employee may possess a range of attitudes towards themself that have a clear effect on the success of learning and development. Consider for example, an employee attending some form of IT training, such as an advanced Excel workshop, which contains some quite complex information. As Carol Dweck (2006) identified, if they see themself as someone who is quite bright and able to learn, then they are more likely to engage with the challenge of learning and use a range of strategies to overcome the difficulty. If, on the other hand they see themself as having a fixed limit of intelligence and understanding then they are likely to give up if it seems hard. They may then either repeatedly fail an end-of-course test, at considerable cost to both themself and employer. Alternatively, they may simply slip out of the course and rely on colleagues to support them, again at significant cost to all concerned.

Approaches involving a psychological perspective are enhanced by advances in our understanding of the brain, memory and perception thanks to advances in neuro-imaging. This allows us to actually see the brain at work and understand which parts of it seem to be involved in specific tasks, such as recall for faces or alternatively rehearsing complex tasks. Other related concepts developed from a psychological perspective include the idea of deep learning – taking time and repeated challenge to gain significant expertise in an area, for example as demonstrated by a medical consultant. These are all aspects with the potential to add real value to the learning and development practitioner.

Other ongoing developments involve segmentation of employees, for example learning and development targeted specifically at high-potential employees or females. This approach involves bespoke tools and techniques provided to meet specific business requirements, such as ensuring an agile and yet consistent pipeline for succession in top roles. It is used regularly in some organizations and has yet to be appreciated in the majority.

I will also consider the growing importance of e-technology in the delivery of learning interventions. Taking a critical approach, I will consider the cost benefit of delivering learning at a distance and consider its use as part of blended learning approaches that involve the use of multiple means of delivering learning over sometimes quite protracted periods.

The relationship between employee engagement and learning and development practices is another area of growing interest. Employee engagement is essentially a management philosophy that aims to develop the psychological contract into ongoing personal buy-in from the employee, matched by a commitment to the employee on the part of the organization, which involves an alignment of the full range of people strategies.

CASE STUDY

Dominus Consulting is a regional accountancy firm that offers bespoke, high-quality solutions to large corporations. It is run on a partnership basis with 12 equity partners, 45 client-facing employees and a support staff of 31.

Whilst Dominus Consulting is able to offer the standard year-end and housekeeping accounting functions it has a strong preference for assisting with mergers and acquisitions. Within the organization those working on mergers and acquisitions (M&A) have a higher status and usually a higher salary. These roles are therefore highly prized, despite the long hours and unpredictability of the roles. However, the organization tends to find it difficult to hold onto employees in the M&A team with employees typically leaving within three to five years. Often, they are poached by competitors whilst a couple have started their own rival organizations.

The founding partner Thomas has long enjoyed the 'cut and thrust' of negotiations. He has an enviable reputation for being highly astute in negotiations and in those long, drawn-out final bargaining sessions where being able to stay coherent and make sound decisions through the night is a valuable trait – his preference for five hours' sleep a night stands him in good stead. He remains a towering presence within the organization and is likely to step into any meeting on a whim.

The organization has been built on Thomas's capacity for quick thinking and building strong relationships with his clients, many of whom have stayed with him for nearly 20 years. Whilst competitors have swallowed up other accounting firms, Dominus has remained, thanks to Thomas's astute thinking.

However, two issues now face Dominus consulting:

1   Thomas is 62 years old. He is keen to stay at the helm of the business that he built. However, a couple of recent negotiations have not been as advantageous to his client as usual and there is a rumour that Thomas is losing some of his 'edge'. These rumours have reached the marketing and HR directors, they are concerned about how to handle this for the long-term good of the organization.

2   Thomas is frustrated by the lack of quality applicants. He has followed the advice of his HR function in recruiting young accountancy graduates but is frustrated that none of them seem able to comprehend the ins and outs of negotiating – which to Thomas are like his daily paper, familiar and comfortable.

Dominus Consulting has an HR function, but no learning and development strategy. How would you advise Dominus Consulting? What do you think are the core issues that they should deal with and how would you go about persuading Thomas of the need for learning and development?

In conclusion

This introductory chapter has covered a great deal of ground. I have considered a definition of learning and development and discussed the wide range of practices and outcomes that are involved. I have also considered the factors that influence the practice of learning and development. The rest of this book will go on to discuss these in detail. Part One of the book is a more in-depth discussion of the various approaches to learning and development and how each of these measures up. The second half of the book is more practical and identifies ways in which you can undertake learning and development for a successful outcome. However, to be successful it is important that you read both parts of the book and carefully consider how to apply them to your own situation, simultaneously influencing stakeholders to get as much backing as possible.

Discussion of Dominus Consulting

Dominus is no different from a large number of professional practices – it is built on the talents of one man and could either fail once he leaves the industry, or adapt to change and grow. The HR function has a number of issues to deal with:

1 *Onboarding and development of professional recruits.* There is a danger that they may be cardboard cut-outs of Thomas, self-selected because they admire him, but less capable and perhaps, over time, less what the market conditions require.

2 *Developing negotiation capabilities across the organization.* This is done through both training and coaching.

3 *Assessing the current situation.* Is Thomas starting to lose capability? Is it some 'negative speak' from a competitor or is the nature of negotiating changing? And what is the appropriate activity in each case?

4 *Strategizing for the future.* This includes the development of a successor to Thomas, or perhaps a range of potential successors.

The importance of learning and development

02

Introduction

Edmund Burke, in his *Reflections on the Revolution in France* (1790) noted that, 'The state without the means of some change is without the means of its conservation'. Applying this to both organizations and nations has been my key theme. Change is inevitable; it is simply not possible for an organization or nation to remain static. Therefore, it is best to be proactive and direct the change to a desirable end point. Learning and development is one way of doing this. It encompasses an understanding of the current status, the external environment in which the organization or nation operates and various tools to support people in reaching the end goal. The risks of not engaging with change at organizational and national level are far more severe than those of engaging. In the previous chapter we discussed the endemic nature of change in the economy at a global and a local level.

This chapter will address these issues at a range of levels, from national through to micro-organizational. I will consider the context and embeddedness of learning and development in order to demonstrate why it is important.

The American Society for Training and Development (ASTD) in 1997 compared total shareholder return (TSR) with investment in employee learning and development. They found:

- An average increase of US $680 in development investment per employee was correlated with 6 per cent increase in TSR the following year after controlling for a number of variables.

- They also ranked the expenditure on learning and development and found those organizations in the top half had a TSR of 36.9 per cent whilst those in the bottom half had a TSR of only 19.8 per cent.

- The firms spending 25 per cent more on learning and development, had a 24 per cent higher profit margin, 218 per cent higher income per employee and 26 per cent higher price-to-book ratios on average than firms who were in the bottom 25 per cent for investment in learning and development.

The ASTD notes:

> The bottom line: if investors were able to gain direct knowledge of firms' training expenditures, they could theoretically exploit the one-year lag observed by ASTD and earn above-average returns by assembling a training-heavy stock portfolio.

Learning and development is just one element, albeit an important one, in the range of tools available to an HR function. Used in conjunction with tools such as workforce planning, performance management and employee engagement it can lead to a highly responsive employee base in an organization that harvests all learning to build knowledge and capability as part of its daily work.

This is an integral part of the ability, motivation and opportunity (AMO) model developed by Purcell (2003) and team at Bath University. They noticed that high-performing teams across industry and differing sectors have a consistent 'bundle' of HR practices that support high performance at an organizational level. That is, the higher performance levels of individuals and teams enable the organizations to outperform competitors.

Learning and development become an integrated part of the business with managers taking responsibility for developing their teams and the HR function acting as resource and guide as well as setting the strategic development goals in line with overall business strategy.

Unfortunately, this will of necessity be a general and generic perspective. Whilst there are a range of core principles and additionally typical areas of value, learning and development is also a highly context-dependent activity. Its aims and the reasons for them are specific to each situation. For this reason, a highly effective intervention carried out in one organization may be as good as useless in another apparently similar organization. It is so important that each intervention is designed specifically for the organization in question. There may be similarities with approaches used in other organizations, but the context of values, goals, industry, size, location and perhaps in some cases even function make a bespoke approach to learning and development a necessity.

Personal performance

Individuals within the workplace perform at a level that they experience as more or less satisfactory. This simple and obvious statement is key to the importance of learning and development. Individuals hold within themselves a set of virtual justice scales which they use to monitor how much they have done, how hard they have worked compared to others, and how much they have achieved compared to their objectives and the broader aims of the organization. With this they measure and justify their contribution in terms of their own personal performance. You may know it as the psychological contract (Rousseau, 1989). It forms a core part of the individual's attitude towards his or her own development.

Other individual elements contribute to an individual's desire and intention to learn and develop himself or herself. A core element, which varies between individuals, is the extent to which they believe that learning and development are within their grasp. Partly, this reflects their own educational experiences. If they have experienced support and a degree of success within their education and prior learning then their attitude is likely to be more positive. However, where they have suffered a lack of ability to attain their goals, have felt belittled or incapable of achievements, then their attitude towards interventions offered by the organization is likely to be both resistant and negative.

Individuals may perceive themselves to be people who can influence others and make changes, or they may see themselves as overly impacted by any changes in their workplace and home environment. This is known as *locus of control*, an approach devised by Julian Rotter (1954), which indicates that the way we think about things directly impacts our choices of behaviour and also our attitudes. Individuals who have a high internal locus of control think that they have a high degree of control over what happens to them, that they are able to have a significant impact on their own career trajectory. Therefore they can be quite proactive, seeking ways to develop themselves and perhaps even being persistent in both seeking and consuming development. The danger for these people is that they may seek to develop areas away from the broader organizational strategy. It is therefore important that as part of their performance management, line managers support them in making wise choices about what areas to develop. On the other hand, those who have a strong internal locus of control think that they are at the mercy of external forces. They may well have experienced difficult situations such as being part of a large-scale redundancy programme, which has reinforced their external locus of control. The danger here is one of passivity; they may well accept corporate development interventions, but are unlikely to engage with them, as they believe that events are so strong that no measure of development could future-proof them. As passive recipients they will not engage with the material, will receive minimal benefits and will for all intents and purposes miss out on the learning, at significant cost to both the organization and themselves.

Certainly this is a core part of the individual's sense of what they should be asked to do in terms of both current and future performance. It is complemented with a broad range of factors including: the culture of the organization; the broader social, political and economic mores; and additionally, the personal circumstances of the individual.

The reason we have considered the individual's attitude in such detail is that learning and development once offered are very much in the hands of the individual. Their underlying attitude to development and perception of the need for that learning determine the extent to which they will embrace the opportunity. It is very much as the clichéd adage goes: You can take a horse to water but you can't make it drink. There is a great deal that the organization can do in order to motivate and engage the individual with learning and development, if it considers the effort worthwhile. Primarily, an effective approach to performance management should enable line managers to identify specific areas for development and support individuals in finding effective ways to meet those learning needs. Frequently, the first port of call is courses, but in terms of their transferability of skill and knowledge back to the workplace, these are perhaps some of the least effective interventions. The manager should be enabled to provide coaching support in order to give confidence and encouragement to employees to develop a positive attitude towards their own development. The ownership of their development by an individual employee is a significant step towards successful enhancement of their skill and knowledge level. This clearly contributes significantly to the capability available to the organization.

National context of learning and development

As organizations operate within a competitive environment, so too do nations. This is important for learning and development practitioners as our access to resources is tied up with our national competitiveness. For example, witness the importance of mobile technology in Africa as a training resource where PCs and laptops are less affordable. We tend not to see this so easily, probably due to scale – an organization is an entity for which we can easily see the 'edges'. Even the largest multinational corporation has competitors, a share price that is discussed on national news with regularity and we also see organizations emerging, growing and dying. However, nations seem somehow both endless and boundless. Our own self-concept is often defined to some extent by our nationality, leading to some of the difficulties found within highly mobile populations. Frequently, citizens of a country may identify themselves by their heritage rather than by their country of residence and import the values and norms of that heritage.

Nations compete with other nations for resources of all types. Witness the flight of the highly educated from Greece to more prosperous countries from 2011 onwards. In an article entitled 'Doctors from crisis-hit Eurozone countries heading to UK for work' published in the *Independent* (London), 18 September 2012, Oliver Wright reported that since 2010 the number of Greek doctors on the General Medical Council's register increased by 29 per cent. In 2013, 365 Greek doctors made applications to register to practice in the UK. The tragedy of it is that the Greek system that educated them will have to wait a very long time before it can afford to educate all the doctors that it needs. The individuals are also seeking resources; they have worked long and hard to start specializing in medicine and with the lack of resources in their homeland, who could blame them for seeking to fulfil their potential elsewhere?

This competition extends across all forms of resources, even physical resources. Finland recently started mining in parts of the Arctic Circle where the receding ice has revealed valuable rock formations. The United Kingdom retained a firm grasp on the strategically placed Hong Kong, Gibraltar and the Falkland Islands. The more frequent competition is for the added-value resources such as skills, knowledge and abilities. These are the factors that can develop a hub of expertise for a location. Once established, a hub of expertise is likely to remain and will impact the learning and development options to a great extent. The case study below identifies the importance of a hub on learning and development.

CASE STUDY

Silicon Valley

In the high-tech world, Silicon Valley in the United States has many competitors, but none can match the unique combination and number of skills required to continue to develop the industry through new platforms and new products. This competitive advantage has developed since the beginning of the 20th century with US navy research centred on the San Francisco Bay. Simultaneously, from the latter parts of the 19th century the region was seeking to grow its own industries rather than rely on the Eastern seaboard. Through the research activities of Stanford University a focus on cutting-edge research was developed for the region to become a centre for high-tech research and development. This was given a further impetus following World War II with the return of a large number of ex-soldiers seeking to complete their education. This opportunity was not wasted on Stanford, which used it to extend its provision of technology education. This culminated in the latter part of the 20th century in a world-leading centre for IT. This was supported by the local legal infrastructure, which developed unusually entrepreneurial-friendly laws, such as a ban on the use of non-competition clauses in employment contracts. This had the impact of allowing employees to move freely between competitors, increasing the competitive landscape and sharpening the gradient between successful and unsuccessful organizations. Those more able organizations with the better products, and terms and conditions – including learning and development – were able freely to attract the best people.

This degree of expertise in a region is self-sustaining as it is composed of a complex web of factors and capabilities. In the case of Silicon Valley these are:

- the climate – warm, sunny and pleasant most of the year;

- a culture of rapid growth and frequent change that facilitates very rapid development;

- a culture in which being an IT 'geek' is cool and exciting;

- a hinterland of experienced retired professionals and consultants to support entrepreneurs with coaching and advice;

- significant educational resources;

- a full range of complementary businesses, eg agencies to hire interim experts, provision of components, PR and marketing consultancies, bars and coffee shops that IT hot-shots frequent, etc;

- employment law regulatory framework;

- location as headquarters of most dominant IT global companies.

This difficult-to-match combination of factors generates inertia in terms of location of the industry and an inward pressure as the most highly qualified and desirable employees move to California from across the world, to take part in the most exciting and cutting-edge projects. This deprives their home base of the best expertise and further consolidates the dominance of Silicon Valley. Additionally, it attracts a large number of small start-ups who have new ideas for the further development of the IT industry. Whilst many of these will fail, it does indicate that those surviving with the best ideas are more likely to be able to access resources, build viable organizations and consolidate the lead of Silicon Valley.

The ultimate goal of competitive advantage is for it to be sustainable, ie permanent. Silicon Valley has a number of competitive advantages, but not all of these are sustainable. For example, India is developing an outstanding technical educational infrastructure, to the extent that some of their technical colleges are more prestigious than Oxbridge. With low costs of labour and low fixed costs they can attract inward investment, particularly with their 2013 focus on building infra-structure – investing more than US $1trillion in transport links, energy, logistics and IT. The challenge for any nation is to understand their competitive position, the emerging competitive threats and how to optimize their position.

National learning and development

Silicon Valley demonstrates the importance of a national strategy for learning and development. California during the early 21st century was the fourth largest economy in the world. This was due in no small part to the wealth developed from Silicon Valley – an industry based on the application of learning. The development of this industry could have been anywhere – but once established in Silicon Valley it is almost impossible for any other competitor to overtake their competitive position without intense investment.

National vocational and educational training systems

Nations must ensure that they have a supply of the skills and capabilities, appropriately spread across the workforce for all of the industries and jobs that they require. This is an enormously complex task as it requires predicting the future needs of the nation, the future shape of working life, providing the vocational educational opportunities to provide that, at reasonable cost and then encouraging primarily young people to take on those roles. Consider, for example, the role of midwives. This is an essential role for the health of the nation – bringing healthy new life into a nation is one of the most important roles to ensure the future of a society. How many midwives will we need in 10 years' time? That depends on the annual birth rate – given the current birth rate, current ages of the population and potential patterns of immigration and emigration it is possible to predict the number of midwives that we may need. Given that target, educational institutions must be resourced and lecturers trained whilst potential midwives should be attracted through school careers advice. In reality, the process is iterative, with estimates being based on current provision and educational establishments and careers services established. However, the planning process is essential to reduce gaps and shortages of skills which could have a devastating impact in an area as important as midwifery.

This is the role taken on by vocational education and training which according to direct.gov.uk [accessed in 2013] is, '"competence-based" training, usually undertaken as part of a job, to learn practical skills related to the job eg business and administration and health and social care'.

National vocational education and training is the process for provision of skills at a national level. This investment is to ensure the economic health of the nation through economic competitiveness by developing an educated and skilled workforce. In the UK this is achieved through sector skills councils. These are state-sponsored, employer-led organizations that work with employers to develop vocational and educational qualifications. In the UK the main vocational education and training (VET) providers are further education colleges, which provide half of all vocational education and training, as well as other providers of further and higher education.

Vocational education is sometimes seen as inferior to more academic education. Historically an academic/vocational divide has perceived, for example, history as superior to IT. This belies the importance and value of the vocational route, which includes the some of the most highly valued professions as such as law and medicine. However, this prejudice underlies some of the difficulties in funding for vocational education.

In the UK there has been an increasing emphasis recently on apprenticeships. There are a number of levels of apprenticeship which approximately match GCSEs, A levels and degree-level education. Workers can therefore learn and earn at the same time. This ensures that organizations can develop employees both in sector-based specific knowledge and skills as well as that company's unique way of working.

Issues that VET should address include:

- Transferability of skills. As work changes rapidly, so the skills learnt should be adaptable so that they can be transferred into new, related ways of working.
- Governments should pay particular attention to providing appropriate incentives to employers who may carry uneconomic employees for a period whilst they are training.
- Quality control of provision and learning is very important within such a diverse sector with provision often spread between colleges, professional institutes and employers.
- VET should respond proactively to changing population dynamics as well as industry dynamics, eg birth rates, ageing populations, migration patterns, etc.
- Employability and ongoing career support is an essential element. The Wolf Report (2011) noted that in the UK the majority of young people who complete vocational training are not offered jobs immediately following the training.
- Comparability of standards internationally should be encouraged.

International vocational education and training (VET)

Each nation differs in its approach to VET. Regionally there are similarities, but each nation has its own unique approach to VET. As learning and development practitioners you may well be responsible for activity in some of these countries, or perhaps interact with them. This overview is intended to give you a summary of some of the key variations among nations.

Australia

Australia takes a matchmaking approach to VET, and recognizes the need to move towards a high-skilled, high-productivity economy within a global economy based on ITC and knowledge-intensive work. Training is understood as a key requirement with relatively high levels of participation and there is acceptance by all stakeholders of the importance of skills. The training system and infrastructure provides consistency and quality but is being used flexibly, with increased uptake of VET in schools.

Austria

Roughly 80 per cent of young people enter a VET pathway after finishing compulsory education. Approximately 40 per cent are apprentices, 27 per cent in a VET college and 15 per cent undertake school based VET (Hoeckel, 2010).

China

Around 74 per cent of young people continue with education after compulsory education. There are two tracks available: general and vocational. The vocational track incorporates one-third general academic skill and two-thirds is defined by a particular occupation. There are 270 vocational specialities and vocational lecturers regularly return to industry in order to be refreshed and update their understanding and knowledge (Kuczera and Field, 2010).

Czech Republic

The Czech Republic has a high level of youth participation in post-compulsory education. The need to reform is driven by the requirement to better align the vocational training system with labour market needs – particularly foreign-owned businesses located in the Czech Republic – and to increase the supply of skilled workers. It is essential for continued competitive advantage that the Czech Republic is prepared to sustain funding for the reforms when the EU investment comes to an end.

United Kingdom

This is informed by a demand-led model in which governmental agencies provide support-funding where market failure is identified. The system changes frequently in qualification structure and implementation. For example, in 2013 professional apprenticeships were introduced for HR practitioners, ratified by the Chartered Institute of Personnel and Development (CIPD) and delivered both by the CIPD and colleges locally.

Organizational competitiveness

We often see organizations as large, strong bodies that can provide shelter and employment in the long term. We do not expect them to change or shift particularly and somehow continue to have an expectation that they will persist despite all evidence to the contrary. The evidence is that even some of the largest organizations are more temporary than we expect them to be. We see huge dominant organizations as permanent features in our economic landscape. However, where is GM? Where is Enron? Where is ICI? All strong organizations which have fallen prey to some form of competitive activity. In order to meet the challenge of competition organizations need to focus on learning and development, becoming learning organizations in which the focus is to continually build knowledge and skill in order to continue to compete effectively.

Organizational context of learning and development

The learning and development needs of organizations are incredibly different in different places. Sometimes it can catch a person unawares just how different they can be. This is particularly important for someone who has an involvement in learning and development, for example a standalone HR professional or a line manager. The differences between firms are almost as many and varied as the differences between people. People may have varying personality traits, for example one person may be a lot more agreeable than another, seeking to please and wanting to ensure the best for everyone. In the same way, some firms are very careful to take a moderate and fair line to ensure that everyone is performing to the optimum, and perhaps even enjoying their jobs over the longer term! One individual may come from a large family whilst another may be an only child in a long line of only children. Similarly one organization may be a sole trader start-up whilst another may be a similarly small organization, but part of a larger federation of organizations.

The range of differences between organizations can be categorized in a large number of ways. Some of them are:

- *Sector* – Is the organization public sector or private sector? If it is public sector then it is managed by some form of governing body, typically for the good of a broad range of individuals and its organizational aims will be focused on providing a specific form of service. Examples of this include councils, (local and regional) as well as NHS services. Private organizations, whilst focused on the provision of a service or good to customers are more driven by a profit motive and depending on the ownership structure may be required to maintain an ever-increasing share price.

- *Ownership* – The ownership structure of an organization has a surprisingly important impact on the whole area of learning and development. This is because the ownership sets the direction and internal attention of the organization. For example, if a serial entrepreneur sets up an organization, their expectations are that it may succeed or fail. Typically, entrepreneurs have a history of raising a number of organizations and they will be likely to be very focused on the bottom line. Generation of income will be one of their top priorities and any learning and development activity will be likely to be focused entirely on that; for example, mandatory training to use a new form of technology. By contrast, a large public quoted organization is likely to be focused on maintaining share price, over the longer term as well as that short-term imperative. This means that they will take a longer perspective for learning and are more likely to be willing to consider interventions with a broader, less measurable impact such as management coaching.

- *Industry* – Which industry the organization rests in will also provide a number of drivers and limitations for learning and development. For example, some industries are far more regulated than others. The health and safety legislation and ongoing associated development is far more onerous in the nuclear industry than in construction, although, arguably construction is also a high-jeopardy industry with its fair share of serious injuries. By contrast, the telecoms industry has a strong focus on maintaining team and individual capability in emerging technologies and there is a focus on ensuring that employees have the opportunity to keep themselves up to date with technological advances.

- *Location* – This seemingly simple difference between organizations has huge consequences for learning and development. It is another factor that is so simple that it is often seriously underrated. Differences in location both within and across nations can have a big impact. For example, the legislative regime varies enormously so an organization in Germany will have very different employment rules and rights, including the rights to learning and development from, for example, an organization in the United States. Where employment rights are stronger, it is more in the interests of the organization to develop its people to be a flexible resource. Where it is easier for the organization to lay people off, internal learning and development may be replaced by 'swapping' less skilled employees for more skilled, particularly in a labour market which is buoyant. Similarly, an organization that is more rural will have less easy access to resources such as local training centres or specialist development agencies than city-based organizations. Whilst this difference has reduced with the rise of technology, it still has an impact. The difficulties of transport in more rural locations are a clear disadvantage, particularly when compared with the cluster effects of cities. There, simple proximity can lead to higher levels of productivity, innovation and 'cross-fertilization' of ideas to improve products and processes.

- *State of the external market* – The market within which an organization provides its goods or services may move at very different paces. Just as some children tend to grow in a slow and steady manner while others shoot up and then don't grow again for a while, so markets can grow at varying rates. Witness the growth rates of China in 2013 – The BBC News (London), 20 January 2014, reported that having growth rates of up to 10 per cent, it has shot up as a market, but in 2013 was growing at around 7 per cent. For the EU, this would be very rapid, but for China this is a very quick slowing down which has onward implications for the sustainability of many of its industries. For example, if construction cannot continue at the same pace, then there is a danger of it imploding as individual organizations lose cash flow and so cannot maintain a workforce, let alone learning and development interventions.

- *Size* – The size of an organization is closely related to its learning and development intention and capability primarily due to the flexibility of its people resources and its capacity to retain employees over the longer term allowing for their ongoing development.

This short list of some of the key variables demonstrates how organizations vary in so many ways, just as people do. However, in order to discuss the importance of learning and development sensibly, it is necessary to categorize organizations in some way. The primary way I have chosen relates approximately to size. This is partly because the area of learning and development in very small firms is somewhat neglected, despite them providing up to 40 per cent of employment by some estimates. It also enables a fairly clear understanding of the different choices that organizations need to make when considering their options for learning and development.

Micro-organizations

Micro-organizations are paradoxically one of the most ignored types of organization and yet are the initial spark in the engine of any market. They tend to be the originators of the more unusual entrepreneurial activities, for example very new technologies, new ways of doing business, new routes to market, etc. Their success level, whilst difficult to determine, is probably low, in part as they are highly resource-constrained. The definition of a micro-organization within the European Union is that it has fewer than 10 employees and its annual turnover is up to 2 million euros. The importance of the number of employees is that with so few people there is little flexibility within the organizational 'system' and the input of every employee is highly necessary, ie there is no 'extra baggage', no spare resources. Therefore, if there are any problems there are usually not enough resources and without very well-planned out contingencies, these organizations can die back as quickly as they sprang up.

It is very difficult for employees in micro-organizations to take time away from the workplace for learning and development, as there is no one to cover for them. Therefore, any interventions should be sharply focused on the specific needs of the business. This may require a provider to take a portfolio approach, picking and choosing the most relevant and immediately necessary of their offerings. These should also be immediately business-relevant and delivered in as efficient a way as possible. In terms of professional training, private organizations may offer one-to-one 'workbook' and coaching services to support individuals through specific professional training, for example in book-keeping or accounting. This allows for the individual employee to work at their own pace without compromising their performance levels. There is often an additional cost for this in comparison with provision at, for example, a local further education (FE) college – but the benefit is in the flexibility of provision.

An added benefit of individual support is that with their noses constantly to the grindstone it is very hard for business leaders to reflect on the learning and development needs of the organization. Needs may therefore go unmet. This is not due to any lack of desire to support the growth of both employees and the business, but rather a lack of capability and opportunity to focus on development issues. An individual, coaching-type approach can be very useful in supporting business leaders here. Frequently, these services may be offered by local organizations such as the Federation of Small Businesses (FSB) or government services such as Business Link. This currently offers a one-stop shop where micro-organizations can meet with an advisor and receive various forms of support, including short-term office lets with additional support in enterprise centres. These have a particular benefit in that there are a number of small and medium enterprises (SMEs) and micro-organizations, usually early in their development, who can mutually support one another as well as providing professional services to one another.

Without these various forms of support, advice and highly focused forms of learning and development, micro-organizations have a much smaller likelihood of survival. They may experience significant difficulties in adapting to any changes in their marketplace and may also find it particularly difficult to hold onto their employees.

Small and medium enterprises (SME)

Small-to-medium-sized enterprises employ a surprisingly large proportion of the workforce. In 2003, Tilastokeskus identified that over 95 per cent of Finnish organizations are SMEs. This may be an unusually large proportion, but does reflect the importance of SMEs to national economies. Typically, as organizations they are somewhat less formal than larger organizations – employing up to 500 people they operate within informal circles where most people are known by sight at least. They are also a very varied category of organization, incorporating high-technology firms at the cutting edge as well as niche service providers and manufacturers. This enables individually based HR practices, including a more bespoke and individually focused learning and development function. Of course, that function may well be 25 per cent of one person's role, so a number of the comments related to micro-organizations also fit here. For example, access to learning and development interventions is very cost-sensitive and also related to an individual employee's ability to be away from the workplace.

This is exacerbated for the more senior people in the organization who typically operate within a web culture. Using this terminology of Charles Handy (1976), they are like a spider at the centre of a web – reacting rapidly to everything that happens in the organization in the same way that a spider can dart to any point on its web that is disturbed. This can give the organization a clear focus and capacity to respond very quickly to changes in its environment. However, these senior people, usually one top person and one or two trusted others, also have a pressing need for learning and development as their decisions immediately impact the success of the whole organization. There are a range of options for business leaders in SMEs. One example is the Academy of Chief Executives, which provides regular meetings and small group coaching with other business leaders. This allows business leaders to share their difficulties with others in similar situations and to share wisdom. They have regular speakers who present on a range of topics – all of this is chosen by the members of a local group. Competitors are not allowed to take part in the same group. This primarily enables coaching to prevent the isolation of business leaders who, when taking decisions about the business, have no one within the business to discuss them with in an objective way. The primary need is usually for impartial observers who can coach the business leader on the effectiveness and delivery of their decisions. Over time, this provides a mutually supportive group of peers who know one another and can provide impartial and knowledgeable feedback to support business development.

However, the learning interventions should be individualized, if not bespoke, offered on a flexible basis and supported with coaching. This will allow individuals to make the best use of the resources available. This is because the learner's attitude to the learning is one of the key determinants in its success, particularly in terms of its transfer to the workplace. The opportunity in SMEs is to provide a more tailored form of learning which participants experience the need for, sometimes acutely, and therefore engages with much more actively. For example, a software training package, delivered to the individual's PC and accessed by them as needed, can be more effective than classroom teaching. Here, what has been learnt during a classroom session will be largely forgotten within a couple of days and so the potential benefits to the business are also lost. The downside of allowing the learner to set the pace and order of learning is usually that they are very focused on short-term, immediate needs and so may not use packages.

CASE STUDY

A look at a small-to-medium enterprise

Jan is a serial entrepreneur in Ireland. Having owned and run a string of organizations since her early 20s she understands how small organizations work. A fount of knowledge, she acts as a mentor for business skills and the local chamber of commerce, where she is regarded as a cornerstone of the local economy. Her latest venture is a highly specialized form of microchip, which is compatible with a broad range of devices. She runs a factory that manufactures the microchips with a staff of 320. There are two primary sites, one for manufacturing and the other, 12 miles away in a local market town, provides the administrative function as well as purchasing and marketing. Jan herself flits between the two, keeping on top of everything.

In the past month Jan has been feeling vaguely unwell. She was finally persuaded to visit her doctor a couple of days ago and is due to go into hospital in the next couple of days for surgery. She has been told to prepare for six weeks or more away from the business. Simultaneously, she has lost one of her major clients to a new competitor, whom she investigated through posing as a customer. They offer a more advanced microchip at a reduced price. Jan cannot see how they can offer this price but is concerned to upgrade her own offering as soon as possible. In the meantime, Jan has to decide who she can rely on to work on the business whilst she is away. She has not told the team yet, but has no idea who she will ask to hold the fort for her.

What should Jan have done to prepare for these difficulties? How could she have made use of learning and development interventions to prepare her team? How can her team best respond now to meet the new competitive threat?

Multinational corporation (MNC)

These are organizations across a range of sectors that can be identified by their cross-border nature. They have significant amounts of their business in a number of different nation states. Thus, an organization which produces and sells in one country, but is registered for tax purposes elsewhere is not really an MNC. MNCs typically source materials in one location, manufacture or add value in some way in other countries and finally sell across a further range of nations. These organizations tend to be large and complex. This in itself leads to complexity in managing and developing the people resource. The primary importance of learning and development activities in multinational corporations is twofold:

1 *Supporting a sustainable competitive advantage.*

  – Focusing on enhancing those systems and processes that provide a clear competitive advantage for the organization. For example, some supermarket retailers have a significant competitive advantage in the collection and use of customer data. Through loyalty cards they are able to predict customers' shopping patterns, enable more efficient buying, provide personalized marketing through apparently individual offers to groups of customers and optimize the value of the rewards system because through following buying patterns they know what their customers will value. This kind of advantage builds up over time through ensuring that employees have the knowledge, skills and abilities needed to conceive of, design, build and maintain such a system. It requires top management support and gives a clear advantage over competitors.

2 *Moderating and enabling a positive impact of the various cultural influences.*

  – Organizations have their own unique culture, which is the usual way of doing things. For example, whether you are visiting offices in the United States, Brazil or the Pacific Rim, certain elements will be familiar and stable. These can be built on signs and symbols such as the logo, filing systems, job titles as well as myths such as the office jokes that circulate about top people in the business. Whilst the local area may seem strange and different, the office will have a sense of familiarity through its continuous culture with your usual office. However, the local cultural values will also be present and it is the role of managers and learning and development in particular to support the integration of local culture with corporate culture in a positive and growing manner. Ideally, this will enable the organization to adapt to and learn from the cultural values of each location at the same time as working to build a unique unitary corporate culture.

Multinational corporations (MNCs) have a tendency to be quoted on one of the major stock markets such as the ASX (Australian Stock Exchange), a high-tech stock exchange which is similar to the NASDAQ (National Association of Securities Dealers Automated Quotations) high-tech stock exchange in the United States, MICEX, the Moscow Interbank Currency Exchange, The FTSE 100 London Stock Exchange and the Shanghai Stock Exchange in China. Each of these stock exchanges is focused on a limited range of activities, with a sharp focus on one specific area of dealing.

The ownership of MNCs in therefore in the hands of shareholders. This can have a surprisingly big impact on the impetus for learning and development activities. Some of the share-owners are institutions, such as pension funds. They buy and sell shares in a functional, mathematical manner through algorithms and are very distanced from the organization. They are less interested in the quality of management and the development of capability across the organization, except as it impacts on the price of shares in the often quite short period that they are holding them. This leads to an ethos known as 'financialization' in which the short-term financial results dominate the organization. These figures may include share price over a quarter, market share over a year, success of new products within a 'season', etc. This has the impact of skewing the focus of the business leaders towards those figures and so engaging the attention of the whole organization on a small range of publicly disseminated figures to the detriment of a broader range of organization-wide targets which build long-term success. Financialization can lead an organization to focus on shorter and shorter time frames as it chases 'good' results, which are more relevant to the success of institutional shareholders than to the benefit of the organization itself.

This has a particularly significant impact on learning and development because results are so difficult to measure and the benefit of the investment in development is garnered over a whole career. This can also lead to some instability for learning and development functions within a multinational corporation. If the results are not favourable then the organization is usually required to react very quickly with some would say dramatic activity – that is, it is publicly flagged as activity focused on raising the results that directly impact the share price. Learning and development is one of the functions that is disproportionately affected here as it is usually not business-critical in the short term. Therefore, any work on building capability across management, setting culture and supporting business skills can be lost in a very short time.

Professional services

Professional services firms vary in size from sole practitioners through to international multidisciplinary practices. They tend to focus on a partner model with a highly experienced, seasoned practitioner leading a team focusing on one specific area. They may form as consultancies, especially in the non-legislated areas such as business psychology. However, where their services are a legal requirement such as law and accountancy, consultancy services will be an add-on. As these services are so fundamentally important to clients, the accuracy and effectiveness of the service is very important and is driven to a great extent by the trust that the client has in the provider. Therefore, learning and development assume a strong value in these organizations.

Much of the focus of learning and development will be on the statutory development of professional skills as ordained by the professional body. This usually consists of a number of stages of rigorous development in the early career stages, including exams to pass and log books to demonstrate continuous professional development (CPD) with very specific outlines. The professional knowledge required as an underpinning will have been gained through education with lawyers, for example, having usually gained an undergraduate law degree, followed by a year's intensive education in law practice at law school. If the first degree was in another subject this becomes two years at law school. This is then followed by two years as a trainee in a firm, following an apprenticeship-type model and then finally the individual has the right to call themselves a solicitor. From now on their experience is measured in years' post-qualification experience or PQE and they are required to undertake considerable ongoing development, which is monitored through CPD points. The Law Society can do an audit of a firm's PQE record at any time and have a range of punishments if the PQE record is very poor.

The learning and development function is much concerned with the professional development of its fee earners. However, it is important that it is not overwhelmed by these needs nor in danger of failing to fulfil its other basic functions, such as developing the managerial capability of the organization and developing the groups of employees who are not bound by professional rules, such as administrative employees, IT, marketing, finance, etc. One danger can be that the organization becomes imbalanced in its focus on fee earners and if the 'back-office' support functions are not also developed then the firm can become uncompetitive due to poor processes. For example, if the finance function is under-skilled, it doesn't matter how good the lawyers are; if the bills are not sent and the payment deposited in a timely manner, then the organization will suffer and potentially fail.

Merger and acquisition (M&A)

Mergers and acquisitions concern situations in which two organizations are combined into one new one. This is often promoted as a merger in which both organizations are equal partners. Whilst this may be the case legally, with the owners each deriving equal value for their half of the organization, in practical terms there is almost always a dominant partner who sets the culture, processes and often even locations for both parties. By contrast, an acquisition is a combining of two organizations where one 'eats' the other so that the identity of that organization essentially disappears.

The learning and development function provides an essential function here, along with HR and (where separate) the organization development function. That role is to help employees adjust to the changes involved, and to support the business in combining teams and processes in order to raise performance levels as soon as possible.

Merger and acquisition is a very risky prospect, with the full range of partners being alert to the potential for difficulties and competitors responding to the M&A with new, often aggressive tactics. It is equally risky from the perspective of employees in both organizations. Employees may see the value of bringing two organizations together, but are still likely to feel threatened due to a perception of loss of job security, a loss which is almost a bereavement of the old organizational culture and also an uncertainty about what the organization will do in the future – is this one is a series of potential changes? Where there have been redundancies the remaining employees often experience survivor guilt, which can lead them to feel afraid of being caught in the new wave of redundancies, frustrated at their loss of working relationships and change of work and also more likely to leave the organization of their own choice. This can lead to a loss of core skills as well as informal organizational knowledge, which is a central part of the organization's capability.

The role of learning and development here is to support the management and leadership in engaging with the situation – ensuring that they are sufficiently skilled and aware to be able to communicate effectively, coach and support employees and also to design the new organization in as effective and efficient a manner as possible. This role overlaps with that of the organization development function, and may in fact be known as human resources development (HRD). Nevertheless, whatever the title attributed to the function, the role is to support the organization in engaging as soon as possible in integrating the new situation and building up performance levels for the success of the new organization. In particular, managers should be supported in developing their own emotional intelligence in order to be proficient in sense-giving to communicate and manage the perceptions of employees. This essential faculty may prevent the development of 'hot spots' of discontent where higher levels of turnover can have a significantly detrimental effect on the organization's functioning.

CASE STUDY

Merger and acquisition study

Major-card and Now-card, two medium-sized providers of credit cards, merged during 2011. The merger was forced by the global financial meltdown. Each organization had a niche lending book, each of which complemented the other. The merger was not between equal partners and Major-card is the dominant partner. Therefore, its systems, policies and procedures were integrated into those of Now-card. This was completed two years ago but there is considerable disquiet among employees who were previously with Now-Card concerning where they sit in the organization, their long-term vision and also their prospects. Both organizations had head offices in regional towns just outside the M25 and each had a different cultural fit.

The HR policies put in place initially focused on bringing the two organizations together to form one overarching culture. This was primarily through high-visibility leadership; the CEO of Major-card sent out e-mails to all staff, which identified the new business vision and goals. This was broken down into practical activities in a series of town halls where employees were free to ask questions and make suggestions. Senior managers then cascaded the inspiring messages through local events to explain the vision, implications and goals for their own teams.

These culture-setting activities set the organization up but employees were not fully engaged in the new business goals. Surveys indicated that the level of anxiety and discontent among employees was higher than expected. In particular, there were a significant number of employees expressing a desire to leave the organization for new roles. Given the intensely competitive nature of the industry the CEO called her key team together to set a plan for bringing the business together and setting people towards the new business goals.

They identified the key issues as:

- A large proportion of employees felt uncertain about their new roles and did not see a clear long-term future for themselves as part of the business.

- The degree of acceptance of the new culture was very variable, with 'culture wars' in one location through favouritism, to a dull acceptance that things had now changed.

- There was insufficient practical training on the new systems and procedures.

They identified a suite of activities to support employee engagement as well as develop capability:

- Practical training on systems and procedures delivered through the intranet and also local training sessions that can reinforce and clarify learning delivered 'soft'. This also allows for practice whilst an experienced user supports employees to enhance their skills.

- A need for a communications plan focused on consistent and frequent communications.

- A need for coaching for managers on how to engage and involve their team in this new situation.

A suite of HR policies was implemented including:

- a new performance management system to reinforce the new culture;
- competencies to identify the new ways of working;
- senior management development centres with follow-up personal development plans, tied into the performance management;
- a new reward strategy that focused on rewarding team performance and engagement for senior managers with a bonus cascaded to all team members based on team and organization performance.

The aim of this suite of activities was to both engage employees with the new business and its vision as well as to develop the employee capability in the business for long-term growth. To what extent do you think it would succeed? What else do you think would be important? How would you prioritize the activities?

Monopoly and oligopoly

Monopoly and oligopoly refer to organizations which dominate the market. A monopoly effectively 'owns' the entire market. Examples of this include the judiciary, armed forces and in some countries, telephony and energy services. As they control the entire market, these organizations do not experience the multiple small cuts of competition. They are free to set their own prices; customers have nowhere else to go. They are, of course, usually controlled by a semi-judicial body such as internal governors and an independent complaints board of some form. However, they do not typically experience the fear associated with competitive landscapes where poor choices may eventually lead to the demise of the organization. Therefore, they are less likely to pay attention to the benefits of learning and development. Practitioners may find it more difficult to persuade them of the value of interventions that build a longer-term business advantage. For example, the business benefits of development related to the immediate role are clear – efficiency and effectiveness follow increased skills on, say, use of IT. However, in a monopoly it is particularly difficult to influence the benefits of development for innovation or leadership development.

This comfort of being a monopoly is also their enemy as critical thinking and focus on results embodied in a competitive environment continually hone the organization and its processes to produce an agile, responsive and efficient organization. The monopolistic organizations suffer by comparison.

This is moderated to some extent by the reach of the monopoly. An organization may be a monopoly in its own region or nation, but may face strong competition on an international playing field. For example, energies suppliers may be the sole provider in their own country, but may have to fight for scarce resources internationally. This may create a two-tier organization in which the culture in the domestic provision arm is somewhat cosy and static whilst the supply arm may be sharp and focused. Whilst the leaders would be wise to seek to manage the disparity between cultures to hold a central, united organization, the distinct cultures are likely to be functional in their own environment. Therefore, learning and development interventions should be differentially designed and presented in order to fit with each of those cultures.

An alternative perspective on monopolies is that they are advantageous to owners and employees as they can garner extra profits, which can be used to benefit all concerned parties. Whilst owners may receive higher dividends, the organization may also focus on further research and development activities to ensure technological advancement, as well as investing in learning and development activities for its people. For example, in the UK both the Post Office and British Telecom have had teams of occupational psychologists dedicated to selecting and developing employees, in addition to the usual HR functions. The ability to shoulder these additional costs can be seen as part of the benefit of being a monopoly.

An oligopoly is a market that is controlled by a small number of stable players. In the UK, the rail market has changed from the monopoly of British Rail to the oligopoly of a few major organizations. A monopoly enjoys most of the advantages and disadvantages of monopoly, for the purposes of learning and development. Network Rail, for example, as the owner of the railway lines is in something of a monopolistic position. It has significant resources for learning and development, which it uses at all levels, both in terms of level and type of learning as well as level of employee. For example, it focuses on centres of learning in order to deliver skills which are common to large groups of employees, such as health and safety training. It also has a dedicated leadership centre, which in collaboration with the University of Warwick provides leadership development opportunities. These resources are used in conjunction with professional groups who provide learning and development opportunities at a local level, on a smaller scale and suited to local requirements.

In conclusion

In this chapter I have taken a broad perspective to consider the importance of learning and development across industry and nationalities. I have touched on variations in organization size and considered the value of learning and development from the perspective of achieving sustainable competitive advantage. In the next chapter I will go on to consider learning and development from the organizational perspective. How can learning and development support human resource management (HRM) and the organizational mission and values?

Learning and development, organization and human resource management (HRM) strategy

03

Introduction

Organizational strategy is the process through which organizations attempt to survive and possibly even thrive over the long term. It involves the setting of longer-term goals and developing the organization to meet those goals. Learning and development (L&D) is an essential part of this process as it involves building the organizational capability to ensure that it can meet upcoming challenges. Learning and development work hand in hand with organization design and development, which both sit within the broader human resource management (HRM) function in organizations. The role of these functions in terms of strategy is:

- to support the identification and clarification of organizational strategy;
- to challenge the strategic direction of the organization where appropriate;
- to identify and engage expert support as appropriate;
- to monitor environmental and organizational changes which may impact longer-term strategy;

- to identify changes required in the organization to meet strategic goals;
- to communicate strategic goals, values and mission to the organization;
- to build organizational capability to ensure that it is able to attain strategic goals;
- to work at an individual level with key individuals to support their development to achieve the organization's strategic goals.

Johnson *et al* (2008) define strategy in terms of choice, analysis and implementation:

Choice

Consideration of the longer-term direction of the organization and its scope

For example, a private health care company may seek to specialize in certain health issues that it has a competence in and that provide a profit, such as private maternity care. Its scope will therefore be a limited population and high standard non-complex maternity care. The NHS has a scope of the whole population and its direction is towards the health of the nation. Within this, maternity care is for all, based on clinical need, to the best possible standard. A charity working in developing nations will also be focused on health, but has a choice in whose health needs to focus on and how to do that. Thus, three organizations, working in a very similar area, vary in their direction and scope. The learning and development interventions will match the scope and direction. For all the organizations, apart from professional training, there may be development in the areas of teamworking and influencing skills, but this will be at a very different level – eg persuading a tired new father to leave will be unnecessary in a private maternity ward that provides beds for fathers, or a maternity facility in a developing country that does not even have a bed for a healthy mother.

Analysis

Specific advantages of the organization

A producer of wine may have a heritage and reputation that opens doors for them. As they have produced consistently good wine in the past, producers will be favourably disposed towards them, considering that a new wine will also be good. This advantage can be used in a number of ways. For example, the organization may consider its reputation strong enough to extend its product range – perhaps to a low-alcohol wine; or perhaps planting another vineyard and producing a different style of wine. Their specific advantage – their reputation – must be protected. This will take resources and is likely to involve learning and development in generating a deep understanding of the company, its heritage and values across all employees and potentially those who represent the organization such as vintners and perhaps retailers.

Implementation

Investigating how the organization can adapt its structure to match its resources to the changing external environment in order to satisfy both the requirements of the market and the preferences of its stakeholders

Consider that a professional services firm may choose to engage a number of trusted associates. They are able to deliver the firm's services to the required standard, but are not employees. Therefore, the costs associated with them are lower. If the market grows so that the associates are needed on a frequent basis, it may be more cost-efficient to employ them. However, whilst the market is sluggish, they are more valuable to the business as associates. The learning and development required in this situation involves ensuring the quality of the associates and that they understand the style, mission and values of the firm as well as demonstrate a thorough understanding of the product range. This may involve designing specific interventions for the associates and including them on in-house development interventions. The essence is that there must be a seamless identity presented to clients.

Reflection

Take some time to apply this to your own organization.

Consider:

- What are the choices that my organization has made?
  - Consider the market that your organization is in.
  - Does it provide products or services?
  - At what price point?
  - Who is your typical customer? What are they looking for?
- Analyse the specific advantages your organization has:
  - What is your reputation?
  - Do you have specific advantages in:
    - business process;

- access to markets;
- innovation;
- brand?
- How does that impact your organization:
  - in its structure;
  - in its use of resources;
  - in its financial health;
  - in its stakeholders;
  - in its people;
  - in its key skills and areas for development;
  - in its leadership?

Broader business environment

HRM strategy is future-facing, considering the emerging environment in which the organization operates and will often concern underlying choices such as which markets to operate in and how to develop people in line with those markets. These are the practical issues that you will now have started to consider for your own organization. As a learning and development professional your core role is to support the business in enhancing its competitive advantage and building its mission, values and goals. Part of that involves taking an active role in the learning and development profession, for example, keeping up to date with current thinking, new technologies, benchmarking how other organizations are delivering interventions and building professional relationships to develop a better understanding of the profession. You may also wish to think about taking professional qualifications such as the CIPD Level 3, 5 or 7 qualifications. Each of these avenues provides a way for you to improve your knowledge, understanding and skill so that you can add further value to the organization.

Learning and development typically sits as part of the HR function. HR is one part of an organization. It has an essential role both in and on the organization. HR employees are part of the organization in the same way as any other employee, except that they have additional responsibility for ensuring the smooth running of the 'people' part of the organization. That is, they are responsible for working on the organization, making sure that it functions effectively and directionally towards strategic goals. Additionally they work in the organization, with similar responsibilities, rights and restrictions that all other employees experience. The dual nature of their employment can pose a difficulty for HR employees. This can particularly be the case with HRM strategy. They frequently know about an upcoming change before other employees, but must be sure to maintain confidentiality.

Internal business environment

Learning and development policies can be used to support the broader business agenda in a number of ways:

1 *Retention* – Retention involves organizations holding onto their employees. It is usually an indicator of employee satisfaction and is closely related to employee engagement. Whilst some employee turnover is useful in an organization in order to bring in new ideas, too much is very damaging. This is because each employee holds knowledge and skills that the organization may need and may not be able to find easily in other potential employees. Learning and development is an important tool to improve retention rates. Equally, an organization where turnover is too low may suffer from lack of innovation. In these circumstances it can be important for the learning and development function to consider innovative ways of developing employees, for example, secondments to customers or suppliers, collaborations with professional bodies or even (very occasionally) competitors.

2 *Reward* – Learning and development opportunities are frequently offered as part of the reward package. The total reward approach advocates including all learning and development as part of the reward package. For example, employees at the food manufacturing company Mars receive an annual information pack that details their basic salary, traditional benefits such as annual leave, share scheme options and the like, additional benefits such as membership of a theatre club and finally the cost of all the learning and development that the employee has received. This may include induction, skills, professional courses, etc. This acts to ground the learning and development as a valuable asset in the employee's mind, which supports the whole range of people processes. Thus, the employee will be more engaged with Mars and so work to a higher standard with greater commitment and the willingness to give their discretionary effort. This in turn enhances the psychological contract, which is the basis for employee engagement.

3 *Recruitment* – Recruitment provides the pipeline for organizational growth through selecting the right people. However, the right people for one organization are usually also the right people for other organizations so that a competition for talent develops. One significant tool that an organization has is offering development for career progression to these people. In fact, for 'high flyers', the organization that offers significant development opportunities is often the one that is preferable. It is down to collaboration between line manager and learning and development professional to identify an appropriate learning programme that is sufficiently challenging and structured without allowing the high flyer to take more than their fair share of resources on the one hand and to not over-promise on the other hand.

4 *Diversity* – Diversity is an important area of strategic development for HR as well as the organization as a whole. The business benefit that comes from diversity involves innovation as a broader range of people from differing backgrounds are more likely to understand the consumer perspective, especially in a global economy where consumers could potentially be from almost anywhere on the planet. This will enhance the organization's capacity to develop innovative products as well as leverage the many new routes to market that are emerging, for example, online marketplaces such as eBay as well as apps used on smart phones to identify price and product information for consumers. This enhanced consumer understanding is important in fast-paced industries where consumers may be very diverse themselves.

Try going into your favourite supermarket in different towns. Whilst there will be a consistency of brand and core food types, eg own-brand as well Kellogg's and Nestlé for cereals, you may well also find very different products relating to the local population. One town near where I live is very diverse in terms of people groups and cultures and the main supermarket stocks a broad range of vegetables and dried goods from North India, which I cannot find in its other stores further afield. This builds up loyalty in the new consumer group – who should also be reflected in the employee group.

Learning and development has a strong contribution towards diversity as it can provide tools for mutual understanding and support diverse groups in working together. One common way of accomplishing this is through the use of mentors. Here, more senior, established employees advise and support more junior employees.

They will explain the culture – 'how things work around here' – as well as processes and procedures that may be unfamiliar to the employee, eg around team meetings and the behaviour that is expected. This individual approach is particularly important as cultural values tend to be implicit and employees are likely to need to talk through their habitual ways of behaving to understand their impact and how/whether to adapt them. Learning and development professionals also add value in identifying the factors that hinder diversity and make it easier to prefer 'people like me' for everyone. An understanding of the blockers of diversity enables organizations to plan for ways to manage around those blockers.

Models of human resource management (HRM) strategy

There are a number of competing models of human resource management (HRM) strategy, each of which refers to specific underlying assumptions, often related to the timing of their emergence. For example, Taylorism or scientific management emerged during the earlier part of the 20th century (Kanigel, 1997) and focused on efficiency of work through measurement. Its underlying assumption was essentially that employees would do as little as possible so measurement of the most efficient way of working and then giving employees a yardstick against which to measure their work was necessary. This approach can still be seen in areas such as Ofsted (Office for Standards in Education, Children's Services and Skills) in educational settings where teachers are not trusted to do their best in the classroom but must be spot-checked and measured against various criteria. A focus on measurement and evidence is a legacy of the positivist movement of the late 19th century and includes a strong focus on cost reduction and efficiency. In terms of learning and development it led to a strong emphasis on skills for improving productivity and honing the efficiency of processes. This was at the expense of a broader perspective that considers the organization and its direction as a whole.

A more recent development within HRM strategy is the understanding of a best-practice approach to HRM. This involves a bundle of practices which are considered to optimize the performance levels of employees and therefore also optimize the capability of the organization.

Ulrich (2010) has devised an approach to strategic HRM that is particularly useful for learning and development as it focuses on developing an intimate understanding of the business. He sees strategic HRM as focusing on four 'legs' of a stool. Just like the legs of a stool, each one is necessary and equal. They all together provide the capability to provide a strong HRM service for the organization. They focus on either short-term operational or long-term strategic issues as well as either people focus or process focus.

The legs are:

- strategic partner;
- change agent;
- administrative expert;
- employee champion.

Reflection

Take some time to consider your own organization. Thinking about your organization, apply the four roles. Are there any gaps? What does your analysis reveal about what the learning and development function should do to support the broader business strategy?

Strategic partner

With a focus on longer-term, strategic based processes:

- How does your HRM strategy support the business direction?
- How does your L&D strategy support the broader HRM strategy, as well as building core capabilities?
- How does the L&D function support the development of the organizational vision, mission and values?

Change agent

With a focus on people issues over the longer term:

- How do HRM and L&D facilitate change processes within the organization?
- How is longer-term leadership capability built up?
- How do HRM & L&D consult and build alliances to enhance organizational effectiveness?

- What competencies are needed for the future strategic development of the organization and how are they being identified and built up across the organization?

Administrative expert

With a focus on operational processes:

- How is ongoing evaluation of learning and development carried out?
- How efficient and effective is the process for implementing learning and development interventions?
- Are data-based processes and analyses delivered effectively?

Employee champion

With a focus on operational people issues:

- How do employees identify gaps in their capability?
- How effectively are interventions in coaching and development delivered?
- What are the day-to-day programmes that your organization should focus on (for example, diversity, work-life balance, engagement, etc)?

Organizational structure and strategy

Organizational structure flows directly from the strategic choices that the organization makes and is a key part of the enacted strategy. It demonstrates the intent of the strategy, essentially showing that business leaders will put their money where their mouths are.

In particular, organizational structure has the following attributes:

- It defines the 'shape' of the organization and the types of business that it is involved in – does the organization have a strong manufacturing arm, or a strong research and development arm? If the former, then learning and development is more likely to be focused on shop-floor skills and if the latter, then learning and development will be more focused on influencing skills, teamworking, etc.
- It defines the responsibilities of each individual within the organization. This enables them to know exactly what they must do and gives a template to understand what skills, knowledge and attitudes they need to identify learning and development.

- The reporting lines work to define the patterns of communication and knowledge exchange within the organization. For example, a matrix organization is highly fluid and allows employees to work with almost any other individual on a project basis. This creates a highly fluid organization with frequent knowledge exchange as individuals contribute to new projects. This is particularly relevant in high-tech organizations where rapid product delivery can be facilitated by good cross-organizational relationships and the kind of informal organizational knowledge which oils the wheels; for example, knowing who has an in-depth knowledge of a client's network structure – rarely needed but essential when it is needed.

- The organizational structure also defines the kind of skills that are required to move up the organization. It explicitly identifies what skills, knowledge and attitudes an individual needs to operate at the next level. It is therefore a core resource for the learning and development function. Often, the suite of interventions supported by learning and development is designed around the organizational structure and its pictorial representation – the org. chart – which identifies who reports to whom, who is responsible for which parts of the organization and also where the focus of the organization's energy is to be found.

The importance of international human resource development (HRD)

In 2010, addressing the world HRD congress Dave Ulrich commented that it was not the resources under the ground, (such as oil and other natural resources) but the critical resources above the ground through development of talent and skills that we need to leverage to build both organizational and national success.

Certainly, with the rise of an increasingly advanced technological society there is a sense that who we were as a people is not necessarily who we will be. Those elements that defined us in the past are being washed away by a new freedom that has been bought by technology. This is true to a certain extent; for example, freedom to work for EU citizens now applies across the whole region. Additionally, through the use of e-mail, social networking, Skype, etc teams can be truly global, to the extent that team members may never physically meet one another.

However, there remain significant challenges in working internationally, particularly in developing employees and teams to facilitate international work. Cultural variations between different communities are very long-standing and likely to be persistent. They developed over thousands and thousands of years as part of our evolutionary inheritance. Examples include how some cultures require more 'personal space' than others, some cultures are more sensitive to feedback and gestures and so appear more reserved.

Applications of cross-cultural understanding for learning and development

The implications of cultural variations for learning and development are both far-reaching and also obscure. They are difficult to perceive and understand because we are embedded in our own culture. I clearly remember one lecture on cultural variations I was giving to undergraduate psychology students. One student simply could not understand that there was not one correct way of doing things. She was sat next to a student from a different continent with a very different set of experiences, expectations and way of understanding what was going on around her. The look on this student's face clearly indicated that our expectation that somehow everyone thinks like us is very, very wrong!

Yet, even whilst understanding that there are differences, we can fail to perceive the nuances of these differences. For example, thinking about personal development for junior managers – in individualistic cultures we see this as a universal good (Hofstede, 1984). It typically adopts a coaching approach in which managers are developed for their own performance improvement. It is available to almost anyone who wishes to engage with learning, most people experience improvement and progress and this informs work that takes a key role in life. How different this is from a collectivist perspective where the individual is subordinate to the salient group. Here personal development is considered a good only to the extent that it builds the community and feeds into the community's longer-term success.

A key question to determine its desirability is: 'How has the personal development built harmony across the community?' This is exacerbated if the personal development involves 360-degree feedback. For a collectivist culture, it is often not acceptable to criticize another. Whereas individualistic cultures would see this as a way of identifying strengths and weakness to direct learning, collectivist cultures see it as rude and unhelpful. It is interesting that as a member of an individualistic culture, even though I have worked across cultures, studied and taught the topic, I still find collectivist cultures less accessible than individualistic ones. This indicates for me the extent to which our assumptions and expectations are built by the culture around us.

It is essential when conducting learning and development activities in a cross-cultural setting to consider carefully the implications of differing cultures and cultural expectations. One approach I have seen work effectively is for the organization to be very clear about the culture that it expects, for example, when working across cultures with differing power distances (Hofstede, 1984). A low power distance indicates quite an egalitarian approach, with more junior employees able to approach more senior employees to ask questions and discuss a work issue. A higher power distance indicates that the more junior employees would not be willing to approach a more senior manager without being invited to do so first and would never question his/her ideas – seeing them as holding authority. This organization was very clear that high power distance was inappropriate and put in place both development activities and supporting mechanisms to enable an increase in cross-hierarchy communications. Initially, the employees considered it another slightly odd imposition from the UK head office. Over time, however, they started to work in a more egalitarian manner, which enabled smoother relationships across the broader multinational corporation.

A further approach is to allow the national culture to dominate at local, more junior levels in the same way that cultures vary across all organizations, for example between the engineering and marketing functions. This approach allows local cultures to express themselves with few modifications, until more senior levels and cross-organization working is required. At this point, managers are engaged with their careers and more motivated to adapt their way of working. It also differentiates them from more junior employees and is clearly practical due to the cross-national work that they are required to undertake.

Neither of these examples brought about ideal solutions, but they did go some way to starting to deal with managing the issues that can become very difficult indeed when dealing with cross-cultural work. If you are interested in reading further about the impact of this on learning and development, a good place to start is Hofstede's (2009) *Research in Cultures: How to use it in training*.

The international perspective is likely to be most in evidence for learning and development specialists where it involves offshoring and outsourcing. These are both strategies that companies use, typically to reduce the costs of production.

Offshoring is the relocation of part of an organization's processes to another country. For example, India has become a centre of IT and it is not unusual for countries to offshore some of their IT functions to parts of India. Given the very high standards of its educational system it is likely that this may well continue to increase. Issues around developing a corporate identity and shared ways of working are helped through the use of social media. These can also be very useful for learning and development interventions to be delivered at a distance. There are a number of questions for learning and development to ask:

- What are the primary cultural variations we need to consider?
- What is the best way of building mutual understanding?
- Should we ensure the development of employees on outsourced processes?
- How can employees be developed to optimize shared and end-to-end processes?

Outsourcing is the relocation of one element of the organization's processes, for example, the finishing of a garment in the fashion industry. Consider that Chanel is famous for the 'trim' on its jackets. There is one French craftswoman who receives the cloth that the jackets are made of, unpicks the cloth and then painstakingly reweaves it into the required type of trim. The jackets therefore have a trim that is almost identical to the cloth itself. This is outsourcing; one discrete element of the process. There may be international implications here, but not necessarily. However, depending on the degree of integration with the core organization, there may be learning and development implications:

- Are there shared capabilities to be developed?
- Are values shared?
- Is learning required for specific business processes?

- Is there learning the outsourcing organization can share with the core organization?

Stakeholders

Stakeholders are those individuals (who may well be organized into groups) who have an interest or a stake of some sort in the organization. They may be quite passive in their interest, but it is very important to take them into account in your planning. Stakeholders are not always immediately obvious, but they can have an impact on the longer-term strategy as well as the mission and objectives of the organization.

An example of this, which emerged during 2012–13 is the power of shareholders. Multinational corporations that are floated on a stock exchange are actually owned by thousands of interested parties who each own a small piece, or 'share' of the organization. These shareholders range from individuals who earned some shares whilst working or who inherited some, to large investment organizations, usually pension funds, who can own a large tranche of shares. There are so many shares that whilst organizations pay lip-service to their owners, with an annual meeting and lunch, they may not actively listen to them so well. During the economic downturn, when people were generally struggling to make ends meet, groups of shareholders rebelled; sometimes led by a 'green' agenda, they demanded to understand and question the payment of executives – which led, with the support of the media, to a broader review of executive pay.

Stakeholder groups vary for each organization, but they can include:

- employees;
- owners of the business;
- suppliers;
- customers;
- governmental bodies;
- competitors;
- the wider community;
- consumer groups;
- media groups.

Each of these stakeholders may be of primary or secondary importance. If the long-term strategy of the business is to satisfy these stakeholder requirements in some way, then it is important for the learning and development function to understand what it is that stakeholders want. Of course, the stakeholder desires may not always gel together and there is likely to be conflict between different stakeholder groups. Managing this is part of the strategic role of senior HR and L&D managers.

There are a number of ways to analyse stakeholder groups in order to understand their requirements and find a way to satisfy as many of them as possible. However, stakeholder interests are very varied and complications to avoid when carrying out a stakeholder analysis include:

- Be careful not to oversimplify your understanding of the stakeholder groups – missing out on a core concern can be dangerous as you could ignore a pressing need.

- Stakeholder concerns change over time and may change very rapidly at some points, eg when the economy changes rapidly.

- Stakeholder mapping is contingent on your position, you should try to consider your stakeholder concerns from a range of perspectives to properly understand them.

FIGURE 3.1   Stakeholder power matrix

	Arm's-length power	*Comprehensive power*
	These stakeholders have an impact in setting HRM strategy but not in the day-to-day management of L&D	These stakeholders are highly involved in L&D choices, both day-to-day and also in setting L&D strategy; they are key stakeholders
	Disempowered	*Operational power*
	These stakeholders may be very interested in the L&D function, but they have no power basis from which to influence	These stakeholders do not impact the strategic direction of L&D, but they have a strong day-to-day influence

High Influence on strategic direction *Low*

Low   Capacity to influence day to day L&D   *High*

SOURCE: Winstanley (1995)

Once you have identified the various stakeholders who may impact the HRM as well as L&D function, you can take the time to decide how to manage them:

- *Arm's-length power* – These stakeholders can influence your strategy and so you may wish to communicate your overall goals and the reasons for your choices to them. They are not so interested in the day-to-day events but have a legitimate interest and should be kept informed.

- *Comprehensive power* – These are core stakeholders who have a great deal of power over what you do. They should be closely involved with your choices and be consulted regularly. If they do not agree with your choices they can easily stop them.

- *Disempowered* – These stakeholders cannot influence either strategy or day-to-day operations. However, they should not necessarily be ignored.

- *Operational power* – These stakeholders have a great deal of influence over what happens on a daily basis. They could make your life easy or difficult and should be fully included on operational, daily issues.

The organization vision, values and mission

The organization vision and values are the 'personality' of the organization, what it considers to be its purpose and also preferences in the way it works. Every organization can have an overarching purpose that it sees in each activity. It embodies and is made practical in the mission statement. In essence, these three answer the questions:

1 Who are we?
2 How are we going to work?
3 What are we going to do?

Vision

The vision of an organization is its primary purpose, or reason for being. The vision makes clear why the organization exists. It defines and directs activities across the whole organization and as such is particularly important for learning and development activities. The vision must be aligned across the whole organization and have an impact on choices made throughout the organization.

Coca Cola's published vision is:

- **People:** Be a great place to work where people are inspired to be the best they can be.
- **Portfolio:** Bring to the world a portfolio of quality beverage brands that anticipate and satisfy people's desires and needs.
- **Partners:** Nurture a winning network of customers and suppliers; together we create mutual, enduring value.
- **Planet:** Be a responsible citizen that makes a difference by helping build and support sustainable communities.
- **Profit:** Maximize long-term return to shareowners whilst being mindful of our overall responsibilities.
- **Productivity:** Be a highly effective, lean and fast-moving organization.

Values

The values identify how the organization will behave – the underlying values that it holds. Values are the pathway to ethical organizational behaviour – where employees make choices around values, then the result will be ethical behaviour. The difficulty with values in particular is that it is easy for a management team to come up with some profound and good-sounding values in a series of meetings together, whether facilitated or not. However, it is when the rubber hits the road and they are tested that things can get difficult. Will the organization stick by its values or take a pragmatic decision for its own benefit? The values also dictate how the learning and development function should go about its business.

Coca Cola's published values are:

- **Leadership:** The courage to shape a better future.
- **Collaboration:** Leverage collective genius.
- **Integrity:** Be real.
- **Accountability:** If it is to be, it's up to me.
- **Passion:** Committed in heart and mind.

- **Diversity**: As inclusive as our brands.
- **Quality**: What we do, we do well.

Focus on the market:

- focus on needs of our consumers, customers and franchise partners;
- get out into the market and listen, observe and learn;
- possess a world view;
- focus on execution in the marketplace every day;
- be insatiably curious.

Work smart:

- act with urgency;
- remain responsive to change;
- have the courage to change course when needed;
- remain constructively discontent;
- work efficiently.

Act like owners:

- be accountable for our actions and inactions;
- steward system assets and focus on building value;
- reward our people for taking risks and finding better ways to solve problems;
- learn from our outcomes – what worked and what didn't.

Be the brand:

- Inspire creativity, passion, optimism and fun.

Mission

The mission statement makes the usually ethereal vision and values practical and down to earth. It incorporates both of them and incorporates a consideration of the organizational strategy. It tends to be very clear and practical as well as usually measurable whilst the vision and values are usually static and unchangeable because they answer deep questions around identity. The mission statement is a temporary embodiment of that identity and usually lasts for around five years. It tends to be adapted rather than radically unchanged, except where the business environment has changed radically. The mission sets the overarching structure for learning and development. All their activities should feed into the mission statement in one way or another.

The published mission of Coca Cola (2013) is:

- to refresh the world;
- to inspire moments of optimism and happiness;
- to create value and make a difference.

The vision and values of an organization tell you a great deal about the intentions of the organizational leaders. Whether the vision and values are enacted and aligned throughout the organization tells you whether the leaders are serious about the vision or whether it is window-dressing. One of the benefits of working across a number of organizations in a consultancy capacity is that you can develop the ability to 'smell' out a culture and its associated vision and values. Employees tend to be blind to these as they are the normal milieu and expected way of doing things but for new employees and visitors they can be very surprising.

CASE STUDY

Mission and values at Borough

Borough is an international insurance firm with its head office in the City of London, next to the Lloyds building. It operates globally in a geographic structure. Its regions are Asia-Pacific (APAC), North America (NA), Central and South America (CSA), Europe, Middle East and Africa (EMEA).

Whilst it is global, Borough is not a widely recognized organization as it operates under a number of brands. It also has a growing arm providing the infrastructure for own-brand insurance products such as those marketed by supermarkets.

Borough has grown rapidly over its 75 years through a mix of mergers and acquisitions with a steely focus on customer preferences and lean processes. It has managed to continue to grow despite its European heritage through a clear focus on emerging markets. It has recently moved its APAC head office to Kuala Lumpur.

Whilst this strategy has been particularly effective for Borough in supporting growth it also allows some problems:

- It faces an ongoing difficulty that employees can become more engaged with the specific brand they are working with than with Borough as a whole.

- The geographical structure has allowed a variety of structures and sometimes conflicting processes to develop.

- Whilst Borough escaped the worst effects of the global downturn by keeping to prudent policies and ethical behaviours, it is passionate to ensure continued high levels of integrity and values-driven behaviour across the whole organization.

In order to address these issues Borough has moved to a global model accompanied by an all-employee consultation and intervention. This groundbreaking initiative was led by the Chairman with the support of the HR director and a team of occupational psychologists who worked full time on the project for two years.

The first activity was a redefinition of the mission, vision and values of Borough:

- The executive teams of all regions were engaged in a three-month-long process of 'retreat, review and imagine', which engaged each region in identifying its key strategic capabilities and mission.

- The executive teams met in a global retreat, which over just seven days redefined the mission and strategic goals of Borough.

- Rich picture techniques were used to clarify and detail exactly what the new mission would look like and how it would change Borough.

- The global structure was also clarified and agreed upon during this retreat.

The new mission was subtly different from the historical mission that Borough had focused on previously. The new mission encapsulated the new global identity with a recognition of the contribution of employees to sustainable customer focus: *together creating a safer, healthier world.*

The second activity was an engagement with the rest of the organization:

- Each employee was invited to feed back their response to the new mission and how it might impact their objectives.

- Focus groups were held by senior managers at every site using a strengths-based approach of appreciative enquiry to identify how each team could use their best to build the new mission.

- At this stage values were also generated following the model that to be genuine values must be driven bottom up. The focus groups used a critical incident-based technique to identify when value-driven behaviour had made a significant difference:

  - For example, in Bogota Colombia, a senior administrator had double-checked paperwork at the risk of delaying the customer in order to be sure that everything was in order. The error he found could have cost the customer up to half of their annual turnover.

  - In Sydney Australia, a local branch manager allowed flexible working without core hours. The resulting relationships built up across time zones enabled significantly improved customer service for global customers with new customers introduced as a result.

- The results of these focus groups were fed to the executive team, which agreed a new series of values. Building on the heritage of Borough, they set a clear way of doing business to support the new mission:

  - act global, think local;

  - precision, mission, together;

  - curious, customer, commitment.

The exec set up a global conference to which every employee was invited. It was scheduled during a regional day to communicate and explain the new way of working. The early results of this intervention indicate that Borough has a more integrated global culture. A survey of product leaders indicated that 78 per cent of them believed that processes were more efficient and streamlined whilst 84 per cent considered their teams now viewed themselves as Borough teams with a more coherent focus on building value for customers and a global team.

The next stage of this process is a global leadership development to support leaders in being the best they can be whilst using an analysis of strengths to engage teams in being their best.

Organization capabilities

Organization capabilities are those elements where the organization has a particular competitive advantage. For example, consider Amazon's capacity to make recommendations when you are buying a book. This use of data from your current and previous visits enables them to encourage you to increase your spend. A very successful strategy judging by the reduction in the number of high street bookshops and also the way that competitors such as Barnes & Noble and Waterstones have developed high-quality websites to match Amazon's.

An organization's defining capabilities may be in a number of areas:

- *process* – for example McDonald's delivers a hot meal quickly at low cost to a specific standard that involves a very highly tuned process;
- *reputation* – for example Lloyds of London has a reputation as a pre-eminent insurer who will insure anything, whilst McKinsey & Company is a consulting firm which has a clear business-focused drive and the reputation that it will not be diverted from its task to enhance the business.
- *knowledge/skill* – for example professional services firms who are engaged as they possess a specific area of knowledge: law firms may specialize in one or two specific areas of law and become regional or even national experts.
- *place* – an organization may have a capability relating to a place, for example ownership of a mine.

These capabilities are important to learning and development as they help to set the development agenda. Where an organization has a specific capability, then it follows that enabling the organization to maintain leadership in that capability is a core task of management and development. This will be through development of the resources used to build the capability. For example, in an organization where the key capability is process, enabling employees to develop the skills in logistics, process design programme management etc will be priorities for maintaining competitiveness. However, of course it may be that these skills can be resourced through recruitment as well as development.

Learning organization

Learning organization is a term that applies to the way an organization 'facilitates the learning of its members and continually transforms itself' (Pedler *et al*, 1991). The learning itself becomes central to the organization's performance both now and for the future. The organization therefore makes learning its central capability and focuses on consistently adapting and transforming itself so that it is never 'at rest' but continually striving to improve, change, adapt and meet the upcoming challenges. The concept of a learning organization has been very popular and there are a number of ways of characterizing learning organizations. However, central to the idea of learning organization are a number of characteristics:

- It recognizes the need for frequent proactive change.
- It actively pursues change and the activities that will enable change.
- Its vision and mission are consistently communicated to all parts of the organization as a central tenet around which change can revolve. For example, a healthcare organization may have a central mission of 'making the world healthier' and all change will focus on new ways of meeting that vision.
- Organizational leaders and senior managers model and support the focus on learning.
- Learning itself is highly valued and rewarded across the organization.
- The culture of the organization is collaborative rather than competitive and employees seek to support one another's development.

This is a truly strategic choice for an organization from a number of angles:

1 The organization must realign its priorities to focus on both 'learning about' as well as 'doing'.

2 There needs to be a focus on what pressing issues will be rather than necessarily what they are now.

3 Employees need to develop a new perspective on the way they work, their openness and collaboration rather than competition, etc.

This involves a very specific way of working that may not be attainable in one go. Organizations may need to shift gradually to this approach in order to keep the business going whilst picking up the learning. This approach clearly has significant implications for the learning and development function, not least because each employee becomes responsible for their own learning with a strong focus on personal mastery. The role of the learning and development function can therefore become one of coach, encouraging those who are out of step to take on a personal mastery mindset and sourcing an appropriate range of training interventions. They should ensure that their work is integrated across the organization, particularly to ensure minimal turnover of highly developed employees.

High performance organizations

These are organizations that seek a persistent improvement on their current levels of performance. They do not rest on their laurels, but instead focus on responding in an agile and flexible way to changing market conditions. They actively involve employees in decision-making and environment scanning to ensure that they are 'first off the blocks' in meeting new requirements. This differs in detail for each organization according to its sector, size, mission, etc. In his book, *Leading at a Higher Level*, Ken Blanchard (2007) has identified three 'targets' that high-performing workplaces consistently aim for:

- being the provider of choice;
- being the employer of choice;
- being the investment of choice.

He considers all the stakeholders in this approach. For learning and development, the key target is to be the employer of choice. For a high-performing workplace this includes groups of practices which separately are not new, but together, used systematically, can provide a significant uplift in employee performance and experience. However, characteristics of high-performing organizations are in essence a development of the learning organization. In 2006 Combs *et al* reviewed all the previous studies in this area and found that high-performing workplaces do improve organizational performance. They included a small range of practices that support the building of high-performing workplaces. These include:

- incentive compensation;
- training;
- employee participation;

- selectivity;
- flexible work arrangements.

Together these affect organizational performance by:

- increasing employees' knowledge, skills and abilities;
- empowering employees to act;
- motivating them to do so.

The kinds of activities that learning and development may consider to enable high-performance working include (but are not limited to):

- town halls;
- suggestion schemes;
- job rotation;
- secondments;
- employee briefings;
- self-managed teamworking;
- consultative committees;
- performance management systems;
- personal development plans;
- ongoing employee development.

Challenges for the learning and development function

The ideal role of the learning and development function in theory is that of a strategic tool that the organization can use to build capability to achieve strategic goals. However, the reality is that it is often a less-valued part of the organization. A look at the organization chart will give an indication of how it is valued. This is important, particularly as where it is not valued it is very difficult for the function to influence in order to add the value that it could. This then simply exacerbates the difficulty and exposes the function when the next round of redundancies appears. Alternatively, it may have an avuncular, comfortable feel. Some functions act as the pre-retirement resting ground of middle-order executives whom mangers wanted replaced with more up-to-date, dynamic individuals.

This is an absolute travesty and where it does happen makes the role of the learning and development professional far more difficult. It is in these circumstances that it becomes particularly important to focus on enhancing professionalism and identifying clear goals that will demonstrate the value of learning and development to the organization. Building relationships with managers and supervisors will allow the L&D professional to develop an understanding of the practical issues that are current in the organization. This then provides an opportunity to develop an intervention that will meet those needs and so sort out the presenting issues. Ideally, this will be a 'quick win' – something which has a big impact but is relatively risk-free to deliver, for example, organizing some focus groups to discuss the typical customer profile so that employees have a better understanding of their role in the organization and how their part fulfils a customer need.

In order to influence the close business environment, learning and development functions need to shake off any negative image and build a clear value-added offering. They can do this by explicitly linking all their interventions to organizational goals, mission and values. They should welcome scrutiny and be able to demonstrate high levels of professionalism and be proactive in working across the business to identify where they can add value.

The tools used by learning and development to manage this are likely to be flexible and adaptable so that they can respond in an agile manner to the needs of the organization; for example, through providing discussions of upcoming competitive challenges between executives on the company intranet with a webinar for those interested to follow; facilitating short secondments, coaching and mentoring as well as business-focused courses with a clearly identified added value.

The learning and development function has a clear offering to make to build the organizational capability, enhance functioning and contribute towards both the identification and implementation of organizational strategy. However, it can only do this if it is itself fit for purpose, professional and integrated with the organization. Having the appropriate reputation and influencing capability will allow the function to add the value that it is so clearly able to add.

CASE STUDY

Giant telecoms network Ciel owns ERN, a domestic commissioner of content, which it uses to populate a small pay-per-view channel as well as upgrading to the primary channels and selling in the general market internationally. It has about 2,000 employees, divided primarily between techies and creatives with a core administrative and managerial team.

The vision of Ciel is to brighten viewers' lives with outstanding content. The values of Ciel are:

- to act in an ethical and responsible manner in every part of the business;

- to take every opportunity to build innovative content and platforms;

- to do business fairly and squarely;

- to encourage creativity across the whole Ciel family

The mission of Ciel is to identify and exploit every opportunity to build and distribute content to gain the majority market share in every market in which it operates, globally. ERN operates within a highly competitive marketplace.

The learning and development function is a half-post that is currently occupied by Gianna. She has a small child and works three days per week for ERN. Gianna has worked in HR and L&D for a number of years; this is the first time she has been part-time.

The stakeholders who Gianna needs to take account of are:

- *Corporate managers:* They set the performance measures for the business, usually in the form of key performance indicators (KPIs) which *must* be met.

- *Corporate learning and development:* They set up a broad range of interventions, which Gianna can opt into, at a cost. This could eat up her development budget very quickly, but the quality is high, as is the status, so employees are very keen to attend.

- *Creative employees:* They seek high levels of engagement with their roles as well as expensive development opportunities, where they can meet with other creatives and build collaborations.

- *Technical employees:* They focus on professional qualifications but otherwise tend to be quite reticent about L&D, preferring to focus on the job and building technical solutions to interesting problems.

- *Viewers:* They want innovative, highly entertaining content in a cheap accessible format.

- *Actors and other 'talent':* They want well-paid opportunities that will increase their exposure. Whilst none of these are employed, their reputation among the community facilitates access to well-known names.

- *Corporate/admin:* They want L&D to build sustainable success against the mission and to please the corporate HQ.

- *A–Z consultancy:* They provide 75 per cent of the L&D interventions for creatives. They have a strong influence in the industry and are quite expensive.

- *Competitors:* they represent fair competition and some suggestion of an industry-based development plan for the creatives.

- *Unions:* Actors are all members of Equity, but otherwise there is little union membership.

- *Ciel:* They want a highly effective, revenue-generating business, which contributes actively to the corporate brand.

- *Ciel shareholders:* They want a good return for their investment.

- *Media:* They want interesting but not salacious entertainment. There have been some recent articles criticizing the reality TV content which some have described as soft porn.

Management development opportunity

Ciel has engaged a training consultancy to provide a broad-based management development activity over a year. This high-status activity has been designed to meet the needs of Ciel's senior managers. It will involve them being away from the business for two to three days per month and additionally working on intensive projects which they will present to a member of the top team when they complete the course. ERN was not consulted about the development of this course and not included as part of the first wave. They have now been invited, and senior managers as well as a number of the creatives are pushing to attend the development activity. ERN will have to fund each place, which could take up to

38 per cent of the annual development budget. Gianna has heard very positive feedback about the activity.

Outcome

Gianna took a fair amount of time to reflect over her choices, considering such factors as:

- the organization's vision, mission and values;
- the competing stakeholder needs and desires;
- her own budgetary requirements.

She discussed these in detail with her manager and decided to send a pilot group on to the corporate development. She identified a small group of seven potential high flyers who would benefit from the development. This group reported a number of positive effects following the first two sessions, including:

- increased self-awareness;
- increased motivation for further development;
- new relationships across the group.

Gianna considered this to be a sufficiently positive response to send a further two groups. However, her difficulty now was that all the creatives were asking to attend so using those already attending as a template, she devised criteria for attendance. Reflecting that she wished she had done this in the first place, Gianna considered that the intervention was very worthwhile and it would have been useful to have been included in the design stages.

In conclusion

In this chapter I have taken a broad look at the role of HR and L&D within the organization. I have considered the internal functioning of the organization and detailed some of the ways that learning and development can support delivery of the organization mission. I have also considered some of the activities that learning and development professionals could use in order to build a reputation, and so increase their access to other parts of the organization. Once a successful intervention has been delivered and communicated, perhaps across the organization's intranet, then others will be more likely to ask for support. It is then that a difference can start to be made and the organizational capability built through learning and development.

In the next chapter, I will take a more individual approach to consider learning and how it can be enhanced.

How learning and development works

04

Introduction

There is a big difference between theory and practice, for learning and development in particular. Other areas of HRM practice tend to have an immediate, if not legislative framework. For example, in reward, the choices around pay and benefits as well as implementation of payroll are both of obvious and immediate importance to the organization and all employees. Any issues in this area will be immediately noticed and acted upon pretty quickly. There is also a range of legislation that applies to reward, for example, in details such as whether pay notifications must be on paper through to minimum wages, vacation allowance, pension, etc.

However, learning and development is somewhat less immediate in its impact and depending on the country and function, there is very little legislation governing it. Therefore, there is a great deal of variability in its delivery. The positive side of this is that individual practitioners can have a significant impact, making choices directly related to the business case and having the latitude to be really innovative in their choices. However, it can lack a good link between theory and practice simply because there is no corporate/national driver for the link. This chapter will address the core issues underlying the choices for design and delivery of learning and development interventions.

What is learning?

Any serious discussion of learning and development must consider the thorny issue of what learning actually is. We tend to think of learning through its results – essentially agreeing that learning must have taken place because of the changes. However, that is to assume learning through results and not to consider the process of learning itself. If we had a better understanding of the process of learning how much better could our learning interventions be? We could also develop a better understanding of the quirks in memory – for example, how memory can glitch when we are stressed – then learning and development interventions can be designed to best enable deep learning.

This section will cover the primary areas of learning theory. It will be a very short summary of the primary theories of learning relevant to the world of organizations. A major difficulty is that most of the research on learning has been conducted on animals or infants. They have significantly deepened our understanding of learning, but should be used with caution among adult learners.

Howe (1980) identifies three important aspects of learning which have served us well in evolutionary terms. That is, they have enabled humans as a species to overcome the challenges of survival, such as accessing sufficient resources such as food and shelter, and also reproduction, thus ensuring the continuation of humanity. Learning and memory allow us to build on what our predecessors developed and so build safer more comfortable lives.

The three aspects of learning that Howe identifies are:

1 *Learning is a process* that is embedded biologically within the brain of each individual and enables us to protect and support one another and also extend the capabilities we are born with. For example, on learning to use a smartphone we can outsource our memory for phone numbers, which previously would have taken up a considerable amount of memory.

2 *Learning is context-based*, that is, it always happens in a specific context and cannot really be understood separately from that context. When we come to discuss measurement of learning you will see that a number of the studies into the effectiveness of learning have happened in false, possibly even experimental environments. How can a test of learning, carried out with an individual and an experimenter measure the same process as, say, on-the-job learning, even if they both consider learning a specific programme such as the accounting package Sage?

3 *Learning builds on previous learning to provide a cumulative effect.* For example, people who found maths very difficult as children, and felt belittled because of their experience, may take that experience of learning into adulthood where it can colour every new learning experience. This is an important point for those engaged in learning and development; for some groups it may be necessary to build up to development activities by engaging learners and building their self-esteem to enable them to access the learning.

The cumulative nature of learning has an important ordering aspect as well. Again, considering the accounting package Sage, it would be impossible to teach this package to someone who could not read, or someone who did not understand the basics of numeracy. It is unlikely it could be taught to someone who did not understand the basics of office life, for example, the use of files and organizational structures. All of these disparate forms of learning combine to produce an individual capable of and (hopefully) keen to learn the accounts package.

There are two primary types of knowledge that could be considered within an L&D environment: procedural and declarative. Procedural knowledge concerns the *way* of doing things – we often think about it in terms of the sort of informal knowledge that gets things done, eg knowing whom to ask about an issue outside your business area. However, it also includes skills-based knowledge, for example how to use Excel spreadsheets and good ways to persuade your manager towards a specific goal. Declarative knowledge is *knowing* things, eg who all the presidents of the United States are, or all the world capitals. So, for example, an individual with strong declarative knowledge may be able to identify the key players in all competitors.

Howe (1980) has discussed the psychology of human learning in depth to positive effect. 'Change and the ability to change are at the heart of all the varied meanings and definitions that have been applied to the term "learning"'. Howe goes on to note a number of areas in which lifelong learning is central:

- adaptation to the continuous flux of life;
- learning for the 'smooth transition of culture from one generation to the next';
- adapting to the ever present possibility of needing to find a new job or career;
- new technology and ways of communicating.

Learning itself happens through a number of processes:

Classical conditioning

This is a reflex response that plays a limited role in learning, but where it occurs it is very strong. To illustrate, a child who chokes on a particular type of sweet may be unable to tolerate that sweet again as they have 'learnt' that it is inedible. Classical conditioning involves involuntary reflexes and whilst it has played a pivotal part in our understanding of learning is less relevant to the business world. Where employees have difficulties, such as phobias which limit their capacity to work effectively, these are usually the result of classical conditioning and usually need some form of clinical intervention. It is used in learning and development primarily in terms of structuring time. For example, I used to teach some complex statistics during a week-long course on occupational testing. We would use reminders of lunch coming to encourage learners to work through to complete the exercise.

Operant conditioning

Another form of learning, this is learnt response that operates through reward so that an individual chooses the behaviour that gains the reward. We can see this happening in a naive form in young children who seek to please their teacher and gain rewards such as a 'smile' sticker or gold star. Elements of this follow us through to adulthood so that token economies, for example in closed situations such as prisons or mental health wards can work very effectively. The individuals are clear on what behaviour is rewarded, eg keeping a tidy bed, which gains tokens that add up to valued rewards, such as 30 minutes' extra leisure. In the workplace echoes of this are also highly effective and are used to moderate behaviour. For example, sales commissions are based on an explicit reward where the behaviour required to sell is focused on by the desire for the reward of commission or recognition.

Operant conditioning is also used in learning and development to manage behaviour during training sessions. For example, early completion of a task may be rewarded with an early lunch break – depending on the delegate group.

Operant conditioning was one of the first forms of learning to be understood and remains as a well-understood way of managing behaviour. It is often used informally, and perhaps without conscious awareness, for example when working closely to a leader's requirements rather than your own gains reward of recognition and promotion opportunities. Operant conditioning is an essential part of learning and development, through managing the learning environment. For example, it may be a tightly packed schedule so people will be rewarded with praise for arriving on time, for engaging readily with the topic. A negative reinforce may be their own confusion if they have arrived late and the difficulty of applying the learning in their workplace. It is a key role of the learning and development professional to ensure that their learning is successful despite any lack of commitment.

Cognitive approach to learning

The cognitive approach to learning involves consideration of thought processes that are internal and invisible. These thought processes involve an understanding of the various elements of a situation and an 'aha' moment when they click into place and a solution appears. The basic processes used are:

- *rehearsal* – repeating what it is that is being learnt, eg repeating road signs to oneself while preparing for the driving theory test;

- *organization* – placing the items being learnt into different categories, eg organizing rules of the road into motorway, A-road and B-road categories;

- *elaboration* – building a picture of how the driving test might go, practising the potential route whilst imagining what instruction the examiner might give you.

The development activity for the learner focuses on enabling him or her to use the various cognitive processes such as organization to understand the relevant concepts, perceive the links between them and manipulate them as appropriate. Within the learning environment there are two ways of designing learning that flow from this:

1 *Deductive learning* – used when there is a clear solution, for example in skills training. Learners may be asked to solve some problems that may be very complex, but do have an end goal. Complex wiring of commercial buildings to provide economic and future-proofed communications may be one example. It would be possible for an organization to design a programme that enables a learner to try out a variety of options to find the optimal solution.

2 *Inductive learning* – used when there is no clear end point, for example in management development. A complex problem with no clear right or wrong solution may be presented to a manager in order for him or her to be able to think through all of the issues involved in coming to a potential solution. This is the basis of a number of management 'games' which are programmes based on reality that

allow learners to experience 'years' of functioning of a mock organization, see the outcome of their choice and be offered a range of complex situations to deal with.

Social learning theory

This approach to learning was initially identified by Bandura (1977). He saw learning as a process of imitation, where learning occurs as part of the social context. Learners observe the impact of a choice made by another and its consequences. They vicariously learn from the other person's experience and imitate their choices where the outcome has been positive. An example might occur in an office environment, where an individual is highly proactive in presenting a potential project to the manager and is successful in both taking on that project and managing it well. Others observing this may well then learn vicariously from that individual's behaviour and imitate it, approaching the manager about their own projects.

This approach is frequently used during periods of change in an organization when champions are identified as individuals who will persuade others towards the change that is happening. It is important that the individual identified is one whom others would naturally seek to imitate. This is a very fine judgement and will involve typically asking internal candidates rather than external candidates. It has been used to positive effect in areas such as diversity awareness where individuals can model appropriate behaviour towards less well-represented populations.

Social development theory

This approach, developed by Vygotsky (1980) emphasizes the social nature of learning. The core concepts include:

- The primary focus of learning is in social interaction, for example, discussing what has been instructed during the break to get a clearer picture and learn from other delegates.

- The more-knowledgeable other is an individual with some expertise who can teach the individual, for example, a more experienced colleague or a graduate who joined the organization a year earlier than the learner.

- The zone of proximal development is that metaphorical space which stretches the learner's capabilities just enough. This implies that design of interventions should build on previous learning and consist of bite-size chunks that learners can manage without becoming dispirited.

An example of this would be using online learning. The modules could be 45 minutes of learning, with the ability to repeat modules and with a short test to assess the learning that has been achieved.

This is particularly relevant to coaching and mentoring. Here the role of the coach is frequently to encourage the coachee to stretch themself beyond their usual level of working; for example, through developing their confidence, or 'framing' a problem differently so that the coachee has a different perspective on it. This enables the coachee to try out new behaviours or skills in order to improve their current levels of performance.

Neurobiology of learning

In recent years we have gained a rush of information about the process of learning through neurobiology. Before this the only option was to teach animals, for example rats in mazes, and extrapolate their learning patterns to those of humans. This is how the ideas around classical and operant conditioning were formed.

Today, we can watch the brain in action using a functional magnetic resonance image scanner (FMRI). If we then ask the individual in the scanner to think about or do something, for example smell a scent or read a sentence, then we can see the brain in action. This is radically developing our understanding of the brain. For example, we know that the brain is made up of millions of long, spindly cells that build links with one another. These links are built when we learn anything at all. The brain can adapt to our situation in this way. Therefore, when we repeatedly try to practise touch-typing, the motor centres in our brain are firing and building connections with each other to strengthen the links. This is the biology of learning and shows how malleable or 'plastic' the brain is. This process allows humans to learn an amazing range of skills, knowledge and behaviours.

This is an area that we can expect to continue to bring about new insights and understanding at the same pace. It would be good for a learning and development practitioner to gain some understanding of this area and keep an eye out for developments that could enhance their practice.

Identity theories of learning

Carol Dweck (2006) has identified two different self-identities or attitudes towards learning, which have a significant impact on a person's capacity to learn. This is of significant value in professional learning as it allows us to support people who self-limit in their learning.

Dweck (2006) identifies two mindsets or schema towards learning. A mindset is a bundle of thoughts, attitudes and beliefs that together make up an attitude, here an identity attitude that causes the individual to say to themselves 'I am the sort of person who...'. An individual may have a fixed or a growth mindset.

Fixed mindset

A fixed mindset involves individuals saying to themselves that they have a certain fixed level of intelligence, they are 'just that sort of person'. There is nothing they can do about their level of intelligence and they consistently reaffirm that in their thinking. The kind of statements they make to themselves could include:

- 'I'm useless at maths. I'll never understand the budget.'
- 'I'm good at languages. Watch how I can translate this passage easily.'
- 'I'm poor at influencing. I will let someone else explain the package.'
- 'I'm stuck here in this job because it is good for my level of understanding.'

The fixed mindset does not allow for any personal development and the individual sees themself as 'stuck' at that specific level and believes that no amount of work could change that. They do not think that hard work is required to succeed, just talent. This applies across the range of talent and can be seen in high-flying graduates who may have an expectation of success simply because they have demonstrated their intelligence in a good degree.

Growth mindset

A growth mindset, by contrast, has the belief and attitude that encourages hard work, to build on previous learning – 'If I try hard enough I could...'. Such individuals do not see their intelligence and capability as at a certain level, rather they see that with support and hard work they could develop further capability. The kind of statements they make to themselves could include:

- 'I find maths difficult. I'll try really hard – I know I can understand this budget in the end.'
- 'I'm good at languages. If I read a foreign language paper daily and watch foreign language TV every day I could become fluent.'
- 'I'm poor at influencing. I must have a go at explaining the package so I can improve.'

- 'I'm stuck here in this job because of my current level of understanding, if I work hard and impress the boss, I could get a promotion.'

Those with a growth mindset see learning as worthwhile in itself and are far better at overcoming challenges. Rather than giving up in the face of difficulties they see a need to persist, try harder and work hard to succeed, which they therefore may do. This mindset can be seen in entrepreneurs who persist in trying against all the odds and then succeed. Those with a fixed mindset may look at them and wonder, 'How did she get xyz?' without seeing all the effort and hard work that built on the original capabilities.

In large workplaces this is often relevant in succession planning. Those with a growth mindset are more likely to succeed due to their resilience. Indeed, they may often enjoy the challenge of a difficult project from which they learn a great deal while those with a fixed mindset are more likely to shy away from challenges which could undermine their self-belief. As they think their capabilities are fixed, any challenge to their capabilities undermines their self-confidence.

The mindset of managers is an important component for learning and development. Some managers act as blockers to development – they are more likely to have a fixed mindset which does not allow for the possibility of real development. A manager with this mindset may be happy for his or her team to learn directly work-related skills, eg briefing on a new performance appraisal process or training on a new project management system. However, they are less likely to support development that could impact the whole person, eg assertiveness skills, reasoning that the employee is 'just like that' and no amount of development could change them.

It is possible to develop a growth mindset and one of the roles of L&D is to explain the mindsets and enable both managers and learners to access the development opportunities and understand that they can enhance their capabilities. It is useful to explain the differences between mindsets and encourage managers to come up with examples of how they limit/extend themselves. This is difficult work as our mindsets are implicit and we do not usually acknowledge them. However, persisting to understand the mindsets and the implications of each can be liberating. Managers will then be more likely to accept development for themselves as well as support the development of their teams. If you are interested in this area, you may find Dweck's book, *Mindset: The new psychology of success* (2006) valuable in investigating further.

Individual differences in learning

One of the most important elements for a learning and development professional to consider is the individual learner. In the attempt to become efficient and effective suppliers of fully evaluated interactions it is easy to forget the individual learner. Within the workplace learners will bring a great deal of variability in their previous experiences: self-concept, expectations, educational level, etc. The impact of this on delivery of the learning and on other learners may be great, either positively or negatively. Think of the 'clown' in learning events – the individual who continually has a joke and tends to undermine activities. It may well be that their previous experience has taught them that they are not capable of undertaking this learning and so their best option is to be disruptive and hope to be excluded. This is unlikely to be a conscious choice – simply a replaying of their expectations based on what happened previously.

Additionally, learners in the workplace are likely to be already highly skilled, and to have taken on board a great deal of previous learning. This should be taken into account in development of the intervention and frequently the skill levels of a learner can be used to positive effect by a skilled facilitator. For example, a manager should already have some skills of facilitating which can be used to support small group work.

Whilst each learner is unique in their approach, they can be grouped together to ease the delivery of learning. An example of this is learning styles. One approach is that identified by Honey and Mumford (1982).

Honey and Mumford's learning styles

This identifies the favoured part of the learning process. They considered the learning process to consist of four separate stages, with different learners focusing on one part of the process. They are likely to engage with learning at that specific point in the process.

TABLE 4.1 Honey and Mumford's learning styles

Stage of Learning	Learning style	Benefits of this style	Costs of this style
The experience itself	Activist	Ready to jump in Keen to have a go	May not consider consequences Easily bored; less good with implementation
Reflecting on the experience	Reflector	Avoids getting involved Likes to observe Needs space and time to reflect	Can easily be sidelined May not access the 'flow' of conversation
Taking lessons from the experience	Theorist	Build models and concepts based on experience Applies structure to understand the underlying factors	May find it difficult to go with the flow Can be perfectionist
Making changes based on the learning	Pragmatist	Likes to plan action Practical problem-solver Likes to have a go and see if their ideas work	Can be impatient if conversation doesn't produce an action

These styles can be assessed using the learning styles questionnaire, which can be sourced at **http://www.peterhoney.com/**. This questionnaire is based on learning in the workplace and so is particularly useful for a learning and development function. Whilst there is some controversy about whether learning styles exist, given that our neurobiology is about building connections, this is a useful way of raising learners' self-awareness – the first step in learning.

Locus of control

Locus of control is a concept developed by Rotter (1954) to examine whether an individual believes that the control for their choices in life is essentially internal and under their own control, or external and driven by others in society. Those with an external locus of control are more likely to believe in 'luck' and 'fate' and are more likely to conform to what is going on in the organization. They are the learners who will apparently go along with the learning, but leave you with a nagging doubt about whether they are actually internalizing the learning. Those with an internal locus of control believe that it is up to them. They are in control of their lives. They may therefore need more persuading about a concept, but once persuaded will be more likely to welcome the learning and put in extra effort to make the most of the learning.

Sensation-seeking

There are neurobiological variations between individuals such that some individuals have a greater appetite for adrenaline, and a greater need for stimulation. Identified by Zuckerman (2007), sensation-seeking varies by:

- *thrill- and adventure-seeking*: a desire for outdoor activities involving unusual sensations and risks, such as skydiving, scuba diving and flying;
- *experience-seeking*: referring to new sensory or mental experiences through unconventional choices, also including social nonconformity and desire to associate with unconventional people;
- *disinhibition*: a preference of 'out-of-control' activities, such as wild parties, drinking and sexual variety;
- *boredom susceptibility*: intolerance of repetition or 'boring' people, and restlessness in such conditions.

Jackson *et al* (2008) has identified that these variations will impact learners, as those with a higher need for sensation will also have a higher drive for curiosity, learning and exploration. They will need to be supported to rein in their curiosity with particularly strong goals, and a concentration on conscientiousness and the use of emotional intelligence to manage their need for sensation. However, they are also likely to excel, as their drive for knowledge and curiosity will propel them into new areas of learning.

Diagnosis of learning and development needs

Diagnosis of learning and development needs is at the forefront of the role that the L&D function plays. It is the first step in building capability for the organization. The essential steps for a learning needs analysis are shown in Figure 4.1.

FIGURE 4.1   Outline of how to diagnose learning and development needs

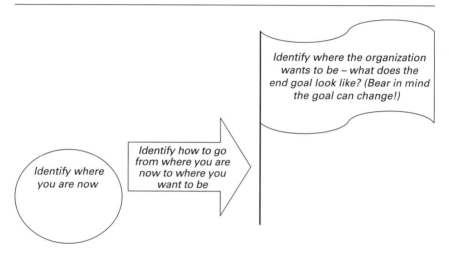

This very simplistic approach demonstrates the essence of a learning needs analysis. It is complicated by:

- *Number of factors* – How many divisions of the organization are there? How many stakeholders (each of whom has a slightly different view of how things should be)? How many nations are involved in the business process?

- *Complexity* – To understand what the goal is you need to understand the industry dynamics and predict changes in the external environment.

- *Opaqueness* – The measurement of performance levels can be very difficult and setting a route to fill various gaps in learning is more art than science.

However, the underlying process is this simple. Keeping to this clear outline will be of use when you are juggling data to identify specific learning needs.

It provides a useful framework to cut through the complexity and consider the essential elements.

Formal diagnostic processes

One core part of the diagnostic process is for it to be evidence-based. It is essential that you take a critically investigative approach to an analysis of learning needs. You need to uncover the underlying factors as well as the precise areas of want. This analysis forms the basis for decisions about interventions. L&D tends to be something of a political football in some organizations and it is important that you have a strong argument to back up your decisions. You may perceive a need for development very clearly, but if an individual manager refuses to release an employee for development, oftentimes there is little that you can do about it. Therefore, having clear and compelling evidence as to exactly what the learning is will be important. One approach to this is known as the evidence-based approach.

The steps in a research-based approach are:

1 *Identify what specific area you are investigating.* This is the research element and you do not know what you will find. It can sometimes be like a fishing expedition; you do not know what lies under the water, so rather than set out into the metaphorical ocean, choose a small piece of water to investigate initially. This may be by function, say, admin employees or geographically, say, everyone in the Manchester factory or it may be by business unit or even product line, so perhaps consumer good or everyone associated with a specific brand. None of these choices is perfect, but they do make the task manageable. When you have completed one analysis, then you can use that work as a template to cascade the analysis to other parts of the organization. This approach also allows you to pilot your ideas in one area with limitations on both the mistakes you can make as well as the positive effect you could have. However, the negative effect of mistakes on your part could be very long-lived so it is as well to work out any kinks in your process in a limited space initially.

2 *Seek out the broadest range of information sources available.* These will vary for each organization but are likely to incorporate:

   - key performance indicators and performance against them;
   - performance appraisal data;

- faults or quality assurance information;
- informal feedback;
- interviews with senior managers;
- employee satisfaction questionnaires;
- focus groups;
- customer/supplier feedback;
- comparison with other similar organizations.

3 *Assess the accuracy of the information.* Check and double-check what you have been told. Check back through interviews and focus groups, repeat your questions to see what other people think. If a specific learning need is widely recognized, what is underlying it and why has it not been addressed previously? Each person you discuss this with will only have part of the picture; through critically evaluating what they say for their level of understanding you may be better able to understand their perspective and its limits. By comparing what a range of people say you will begin to gain an in-depth picture of the learning need and also the best way to address it.

4 *Assess the relevance of the information to organizational context.* It is always important to differentiate between the information that concerns an individual's preferences and that which will benefit the organization as a whole. For example, you may have picked up a great deal from an interview about the importance of one area, say, financial understanding. This may be important at a generic level of understanding the importance of budgets and perhaps the actual budget levels themselves. However, this individual may be very interested in the financial aspects of the organization, but that does not mean that it is relevant for everyone. It is important for the acceptability and reliability of the analysis to take a critical perspective. Ask yourself:

- Has that particular element come up elsewhere?
- Does it contribute to the business goals?
- Is it part of a broader element?
- Does it complement where we are heading as an organization?

5 *Assess the feasibility of the information given organizational context.* The area identified may be relevant and important, but does the organization have the capability to address it? For example, if the organization is in a period of retrenchment and is in the process of redundancies, a large-scale programme on innovation may be inappropriate. Therefore, the finding of your research should be considered in the light of what will be acceptable to the organization. It will be helpful here to think through the culture of the organization as well as its context. For example, what is its approach to succession planning? If there is a rigid structure of succession planning, within a culture of moderately paced development, then a talent management programme focusing on the stars of the future will need to be handled exceedingly carefully, otherwise in a fast-moving, highly competitive environment, a development intervention on mindfulness – whilst very useful in preventing burnout – may be culturally difficult.

6 *Determine whether available information is adequate for sound decision-making.* Finally, consider the extent to which the information you have gathered is sufficient basis for decision-making. Consider the realities of the budget and what other claims there are on the budget. Exactly what information do decision-makers need? Options available to you are:

   - provide a summary of the needs identified;
   - clarify the need precisely and demonstrate the evidence available;
   - indicate the implications of not meeting the learning need;
   - rank-order the learning needs identified from most to least essential;
   - source costings to address each of the learning needs;
   - identify alternative ways of meeting the needs;
   - ensure that all of the above are placed in the context of future and current business requirements;
   - above all, consider your information from the perspective of the decision-makers and present it in a way that is easiest for them to make the decision.

Informal diagnostic processes

Informal diagnostic processes are useful as an initial scoping exercise to understand what sort of learning needs may be present in the organization. They are similar to sticking a wet finger in the air to judge the direction and strength of the wind. They usually tend to involve some form of HR team meeting, perhaps a brainstorming of the known learning needs along with a review of what has been offered recently.

If there has been a rigorous assessment of learning needs in the last couple of years an informal review is appropriate as an initial check of how things have been going. The danger with an informal diagnostic process is that there is a real temptation to stop there! Once some ideas are on paper, with a rough idea of what is meant by them, then it can seem that the job is done. However, the danger of this is that only the obvious learning needs, usually those that have been successfully addressed previously, are included. These will exclude the potentially essential learning needs that are being experienced in other parts of the business. For example, there may be an aggressive new competitor who only some salespeople have yet encountered who needs responding to immediately and there may be learning associated with that, eg around technical capability or processes for speed of delivery. For the sake of the health of the organization the learning needs should be carefully analysed and understood.

Individual informal diagnosis

Informal diagnosis of learning needs happens as an ongoing iterative process. It may be related to situations where there is less formal development, or by contrast, where an employee feels stifled by an overly regimented learning and development regime. At times, it can feel to learners that they are like sausages being produced in a uniform manner by a sausage machine – ie the learning and development function. We need to balance an expensive bespoke approach with more cost-effective group approaches. When an individual feels that they could have got more out of an event, it may be a signal that things need to change. An individual's informal learning may be exactly the level that we need.

Perspective of the learning and development practitioner

It is also essential to consider your own perspective on the learning needs. For example, as a corporate worker you may have a particularly central perspective, which sees learning needs through the lens of the corporate organization's objectives.

However, if you are closer to the line, perhaps operating as a business partner, your perspective may reflect that of your line managers. In each instance your view of the real underlying development need as well as its importance may be very different. For example, in a manufacturing company there may have been feedback from customers about quality levels. If you are a corporate specialist and you know that your organization has zero faults as a key goal then the impact on the customer and its impact on onward marketing may be uppermost in your mind. Alternatively, if your perspective is that of the business partner, you may be more interested in coaching skills for an overly directive manager whose team is responding to heavy-handed tactics with subversion, ignoring faults in their part of the process. Lee (1997) identified four forms of development, each of which is directed via a differing perspective:

1 *Maturation* – This involves a predetermined stage-like progression with an end point. It links closely to change management and empowerment. The organization is a like a living thing with its structures and processes able to be completely understood. Development of senior managers through succession-planning structures is one of the approaches which emerges from this perspective. An end point of a more senior role is identified and managers are developed to be able to 'fit' that role and take on the role effectively when the current incumbent departs.

2 *Shaping* – People are perceived as tools that can be shaped to fit the organization. An example of this can be found in graduate recruitment and development. Young graduates are typically recruited, not for their immediate knowledge but for their intelligence and thinking skills, which with a few years of shaping and development will be of significant value to the organization. They are not necessarily professionals in any one function but typically develop into a functional manager through a programme of blended learning and ongoing development through socializing into the organization, coaching, work experience, etc. This shaping may produce a 'type' of manager who fits the organizational profile and is highly embedded into organizational life. For this reason, this perspective works most effectively in large organizations that have the 'space' to accommodate 'shaped' graduate without the difficulties of clones that can occur.

3 *Voyage* – Here, the primary perspective is of a lifelong journey in which the learner sets their own terms of reference and development of the self with little regard for organizational objectives. This is most

often observed when the locus of a career is professional. For example, a trainee accountant may appear to be highly engaged with the organization and keen to progress in their career. An organization can be very disappointed when these highly trained professionals, who have had a large amount of resources poured into them, choose to leave the organization. Their perspective of a voyage is that their own terms of reference are their career identity as an accountant, which for a time overlapped with being an employee in your organization.

4 *Emergent* – This perspective considers neither a known end point such as a specific goal of development, nor a clear identity for the individual against which to plan development; rather they see themself through the eyes of others with whom they interact. This makes it a messy approach in which the social perception of oneself develops from interactions with others. Perhaps the most realistic perspective, this is often approached using open-ended coaching, which seeks to enhance performance through development of identity and self-awareness. Expensive and often lengthy, it is a useful intervention for senior managers who operate with a significant degree of ambiguity and must forge their own paths.

The range of learning and development interventions

The primary focus of any learning and development intervention is to enable learning. It is easy to focus on the observable elements of our work, that is the courses, sessions, e-learning materials, etc. However, the real work is in understanding what it is the organization needs to develop and facilitating that learning in order to effectively grow the human capital of an organization. Therefore, there are almost as many ways of learning as there are learners.

However, they can be grouped along a number of dimensions:

- *Formal to informal.* Learning may be a prerequisite, for example induction learning is often a formal requirement that involves some form of classroom and presentations concerning organization policies and procedures. Following that, the informal learning of how things really happen in the organization takes place through experience and conversation with peers.

- *Group or individual.* Learning may be focused on a group of similar learners who undertake an often quite protracted learning experience. For example, graduates for the first couple of years of their career on a graduate training scheme will receive group-based learning. Senior managers, executives and knowledge workers frequently receive individual one-to-one learning, often through mentoring.

- *Structured or unstructured.* Some interventions, particularly those that demonstrate learning towards a qualification, will involve more structured learning, perhaps in some form of classroom with clear outcomes. At the other end of the scale, learners can access learning at will in order to meet the needs they are experiencing.

- *Programmes and planned events.* One of the core types of structured programme is a product and services module. Often used as part of an induction this is typically a series of short courses that aim to inform employees about the range of products and services that the organization provides. A staple of many learning and development functions, it has a number of benefits:

  - It enables employees to fully understand sources of revenue for the organization and their place in that provision. Typically an understanding of the value of your own contribution is a key part of engagement, which encourages discretionary effort from the employee.

  - Employees are better able to understand how to support the organization when they appreciate the broader organizational picture.

  - The costs are generally lower than some interventions as they are led by internal product-leaders.

  - When a course is given to a multifunctional group, innovative ideas and tacit learning can sometimes be exchanged as practicalities around the product are discussed.

  - It can give different parts of the organization a better appreciation of one another.

Informal learning

Informal and unstructured activities and projects provide regular opportunities for learning and development. They enable employees to encounter new experiences and challenges and so develop new skills. Learning is a process that is primarily internal to the individual and cannot be forced. Even in a formal training session, it is entirely possible for an individual to come away having learnt almost nothing. This is because the choice to learn rests with the individual. Therefore motivation to encourage an individual to engage with learning is a very important area. This also indicates that learning can come from surprising quarters and as Smith and Sadler-Smith (2006) note, it is a naturalistic process, which is frequently unpredictable or unplanned. It can occur at any moment and can lead to unforeseen consequences. This synergy allows the processual approach to organizing, which enables the organization to develop in ways that are appropriate to the changing environment. It allows an iterative gradual response to developments in the internal and external environments, which provides an ongoing adaptation that acts to support long-term sustainable performance.

Informal learning can happen in a number of ways. Honey and Mumford (1982) note three specific ways that employees may benefit from experiential learning:

1 *Intuitively* – here employees are learning on the job and may not fully acknowledge that they are learning, or fully understand what they are learning. For example, understanding their element of organizational processes as they encounter them. This enables them to work more efficiently, even though they may have no sight of the further reaches of the process they are engaged in.

   This is an area that can be encouraged by learning and development professionals, for example through the development of easy-to-access organizational information such as organization charts, details on product, etc which the employee could access easily at will. This encourages a culture of constant learning, which is particularly effective as it is built at the point of need.

2 *Incidental learning* – these are often incidents or experiences that employees encounter and which they actively notice, reflect upon and absorb the lessons available. This is often relevant to learning to adapt to organizational culture. People are highly attuned to social responses and will rapidly pick up when a behaviour is deemed unacceptable. For example, in one organization with a highly focused performance culture, which is nevertheless very egalitarian and uncompetitive, one employee overtly competing with another will be recognized. The subtly negative response of co-workers will be noted

and acted upon by reducing any urge towards competitive behaviour in observing colleagues. Unfortunately, the highly competitive employee may be so engaged in the competition that he or she does not notice the disapproval and may need overt measures such as a conversation with his or her manager to counteract the unacceptable behaviour.

The learning and development function has a clear role to play here in the encouragement of reflection. This is an often undervalued skill which could be cascaded through managers and supervisors. It enables individuals to capture the learning that they have encountered and consciously decide how to use it. A good example of this is with graduate employees who are asked to keep a learning log as part of their development. It should include both 'official' learning as well as confusing incidents that will usually make sense when they reflect on them and discuss them with a mentor.

3 *Prospective approach* – This assumes that the employee is motivated and keen to learn and, like a miner, is prospecting for opportunities to learn and develop themself. Activities that they may undertake include seeking feedback on project work, volunteering for new work which is outside their usual comfort zone, and asking to support other employees who are working in areas that they are interested in. This self-directed form of learning tends to be particularly effective as the employee themself is so highly motivated. If it can be built retrospectively into organizational processes, for example through the performance management system, then the organization can also benefit from this learning. There is a danger that if it is not recognized in some formal way that it will not be acknowledged and the employee will become disheartened and cease his or her active approach to learning. For example, it could be incorporated into the self-managed learning identified above.

This approach to learning appears to be a gift for the learning and development function. Certainly, these individuals can become powerful champions for learning and development. They frequently tend to be promoted ahead of peers as they are driving their own learning at a faster pace. However, they can also be needy and it is important to ensure that they are not the source of friction in their hunger for more than their fair share of the learning budget.

Informal learning is efficient, cost-effective, highly adaptable and directed by employees. In some organizational cultures it may comprise the majority of your learning, as for example in fast-paced development organizations with highly motivated knowledge workers, where each one is keen to maximize their understanding and all are focused on clear goals such as product development. However, these organizations are few and far between. Informal learning is to be welcomed and supported, but should also be incorporated into broader organizational processes as far as possible. This is because the learning and development in organizations is directed towards building a stronger organization. Uncontrolled informal learning may start to develop the organization away from strategic goals and therefore it should be moderated in some way. Highly valuable, there is a danger of quashing it – so gentle adaptation and management towards learning with a clear business benefit is ideal.

Knowledge management

This is one of the core functions of learning and development. Knowledge management refers to the capacity of the organization to generate and pre-serve knowledge within its boundaries. Knowledge can include: customer information, intellectual property, understanding of organizational processes and procedures and organization charts.

There are a number of different levels of knowledge, each with differing value:

- *data* – single pieces of information, collected together, eg lists of telephone numbers and e-mail addresses.
- *information* – data that have been added to in some way, eg lists of telephone numbers and e-mail addresses for specific client groups in a sales account executive's phone;
- *knowledge* – information that has been manipulated to have added value. For example, the list of telephone numbers and e-mail addresses, with relevant personal information, lists of last orders and best times to call as used by the sales account executive;
- *explicit knowledge* – ie that which is made clear to everyone, perhaps through being written down, eg the dates of the last sales call;
- *tacit knowledge* – ie that which is understood in various parts of the organization, usually intuitively and usually in employees' heads. It includes knowledge that makes organizational processes run smoothly, such as how to approach a customer when the sales account executive makes a call.

This example demonstrates that knowledge is not always objective and can be managed differently by different people. It is usually embedded within organizational practice. The development and retention of this knowledge is a core part of the role of learning and development. This can be achieved in myriad ways, including communities of practice, developing high-performance work culture or learning organization, through the use of organizationally based social media or works committees.

Double loop learning

Double loop learning is one of the primary methods of knowledge management. Developed as a concept by Chris Agyris (Agyris and Schön, 1974), it is a step further on from single loop learning.

Single loop learning involves *choice–feedback–adapt–choice* to improve outcome. It involves increasing effort to ensure that a goal can be met. For example in an organization with high turnover, HR professionals can work hard to recruit the right people, ensuring that there are good recruitment tools that reach out to a large population of appropriate candidates and that selection techniques are rigorous.

However, it is when they question the goal – of recruiting people to fill the gap – that double loop learning happens. By reviewing the goal and questioning whether that goal was the key to solving the problem of turnover, the HR professional may take a broader look at the situation. This is more likely to reveal the cause of high turnover, perhaps low salaries, or organizational issues such as an overly directive culture.

Through using double loop learning the underlying causes of issues can be unearthed so that effort can be applied more effectively to bring about a better degree of organizational success.

Psychological contract

The psychological contract is a concept that underlies a great deal of the activity undertaken by HR professionals and by the learning and development function in particular. It refers to the understanding that develops between organization and employee – an unspoken set of expectations that each party has with regards to the other. For example, the employee may consider it reasonable for the organization to allow him or her to leave at very short notice for a family emergency. The organization likewise may regard it as reasonable to expect the employee to work a couple of extra hours if there has been some sort of crisis, such as machinery breaking down. These mutual expectations are unwritten and a two-way unspoken definition of what is understood as reasonable. Where both parties share a mutual understanding of what is reasonable, the contract is described as healthy. This typically means that the employee and organization have both been honest and straightforward in their mutual dealings, following through on promises and acting in a predictable manner.

The importance of this in learning and development is that the healthier the psychological contract, the more likely it is that motivation and so performance levels will be strong. Learning and development initiatives are a key input to a healthy psychological contract.

Employee engagement

Employee engagement is a concept that describes the employees' relationship with the organization. It is an important concept as engaged employees are those who are willing to go the extra mile for the organization. They are willing to give discretionary effort to make sure that the job is done well. The CIPD recognizes that engaged employees are engaged at a number of levels:

- *cognitive* – they enjoy their work and consider ways to perform better;
- *affective* – they relate well to others in the organization, seeking to support them in their work as well as discuss improvements to the ways of working;
- *physical* – they give significant physical effort in their roles.

There are a number of enablers and drivers of engagement. One of the key enablers is authenticity and integrity of leaders. This is played out in organizational processes that demonstrate that managers mean what they say. A core part of this is in people processes and in learning and development. Employees who see a future for themselves in the organization and can access development are more likely to be engaged and so add value for the organization.

Managing group development

Graduates

Graduate development focuses on the cohort of graduate trainees recruited, usually directly from university via the 'milkround'. They are typically selected for their potential onto formal graduate training programmes. These programmes last around 18 months to three years and enable the graduates to rapidly develop business understanding in order to work at first line manager level by the end of the training scheme. Development is usually intense and involves a blend of formal courses, job rotation, mentoring, coaching, professional qualifications, structured project work, etc.

Managers

Management and leadership development is an area that is usually understood as separate from employee development. It typically focuses on those areas that build strategic capability for the organization as a whole. It involves learning focused typically on the organization's competencies and usually covers the full range of management tasks including team leadership, coaching management, finance, commercial awareness, etc. Large organizations may use a structured and formal approach to provide specific interventions for managers at a certain level. This ensures that their managers receive an education in management. This can be recognized, for example by the Chartered Management Institute (CMI) as a formal qualification in management through the qualifications framework.

Apprentices

Apprentices receive learning as a formal part of their contract. Usually young school-leavers in their first employed role, they will typically attend college a couple of days a week. They are paid a low salary and in return receive significant learning and development over a time period of around two years. This aims to provide them with the qualifications they need to work effectively work in a trade. In 2013 there was a major push towards the provision of apprenticeships.

Executives

Executives here are usually members of the top team or their direct reports, and they will usually have the title 'director' in their role. The development of executives within an organization can have a disproportionate benefit as their decisions and choices have a major impact on the organization as a whole. Therefore, it is usually worth putting a lot of thought and effort into their development. However, there can be an inference that development is a sign of inability and may therefore easily be rejected by executives who do not wish to appear weak to their peers. It is therefore important to pitch the development positively and discuss it as enhancing already strong capabilities. Clearly, this is not always the case and where an executive has the insight to understand his or her own areas for development, learning and development can provide a very significant benefit.

There are some typical difficulties which executives experience on promotion:

- In more junior roles executives would have followed a programme set by others, now they must set the programme themselves. Sitting at a desk with no one else telling you what to do can be disorientating and they may take some time to adjust to this new perspective.

- More junior roles have a strong focus on short-term goals achievement and often executives have been promoted as they are task-focused and capable of pushing a team to achieve difficult short-term goals. However, at an executive level a broad range of perspectives needs to be balanced, over the longer term. This involves changes in thinking style, communication style and process.

- Often executives have previously used an autocratic leadership style, which is likely to be less effective when working with senior levels of an organization. They need to develop a more persuasive approach to generate a consensus concerning a project among their peers and direct reports.

- Executives are usually focused on both the internal working of the organization as well as its public face. This may involve more external relationships at industry level, for example sitting on industry committees, building relationships with organizational shareholders, corporate entertainment and responding to the media. Each of these is highly skilled and executives may need support to develop the communication skills required.

Development of executives is usually individual, via a coaching relationship, perhaps supported with gaining insight through a 360-degree feedback process. It may also be supported with an educational approach, for example specialist leader programmes at a business school. The pattern of development for each executive is likely to be individual and will usually focus on enhancing their self-awareness and then supporting them in developing on areas of their choice.

Top team

A top team is the executive for the organization that is tasked with making the core strategic decisions. Highly exposed by the public nature of their role, top teams are also typically very political and the members do not usually know one another particularly well. Plagued therefore by mutual lack of confidence, it is difficult for the team to function.

Development interventions for top teams primarily address these issues. However, because of issues around status and confidentiality all interventions should be carried out by external suppliers. These should be recommended and should be assessed for quality, with references being taken from other organizations similar to yours, with whom they have worked.

High flyers

High flyers are those high potential employees who could provide a significant resource for the organization through their own capabilities. They may come from a diverse range of backgrounds but tend to have a set of characteristics defined by Yapp (2005):

1 *Constant learning.* They have a consistently strong desire to learn and keep on learning. They wish to stay ahead of the curve in a number of areas and have an almost insatiable desire to increase their own understanding, knowledge, skills and behaviours. This extends to their leisure activities, what is sometimes known as their hinterland where again they seek further understanding and capability, perhaps in music, sports or other leisure pursuits.

Locke and Latham (1990) identified a theory of motivation relevant to high flyers known as *goal setting theory*. This indicates that the goals that individuals set for themselves are based on their own internal intentions, the achievements that they set for themselves. This is one area in which high flyers are set apart from other employees as they are more likely to have a learning orientation rather than a goal orientation. An employee may have a goal based on a key performance indicator (KPI) that they have received during their performance appraisal. This may be to increase footfall (number of customers) in a store, or increase the average spend per customer. This is a performance orientation and the employee who achieves this will be a valuable asset to the organization.

Where it differs for high flyers is that their learning orientation will take the same goals and seek to learn as much as possible from them; for example, why customers make specific choices, how merchandising could be adapted to increase sales, why that target was set, whether the price point could be adapted, how to source goods differently to increase the sales margin, etc. That is, their underlying goal is to consistently learn and enhance their own performance levels. When they change jobs, it is often as much to do with new learning opportunities as it is to do with the organization they are leaving or the new responsibilities that they will have.

2 *Emotional intelligence and agility.* High flyers have a capacity to understand themselves and others, both implicit and explicit preferences and to control and adapt their behaviour appropriately. They are also likely to be genuine team players with a strong desire to support and develop the whole team as well as themselves.

They also consistently scan the environment and are adept at spotting anomalies and responding to them. These may be moments that happen very suddenly without warning and are potentially career limiting. For example, in a car journey an individual may become frustrated about a series of delays and hold ups and decide to cut up another car. As the cars pass the driver realizes to their horror that it is their boss's boss – who looks directly at them, and scowls! The high flyer will respond very quickly with an apology, mouthing 'sorry', trying to pull over and later sending an e-mail which undercuts the difficulty appropriately using the organizational culture as a guide; it may vary from, 'Sorry – I was trying to hit you' (most likely to be a macho, jokey professional services firm!) to, 'Sorry – I was desperately late for "x" client' (most likely to be a supplier of high-value goods or services, such as a provider of hi-tech equipment to a few key accounts).

3 *Intelligence*
High flyers have a strong engine, ie they are able to think in a highly complex manner and to manage a number of competing issues simultaneously. They may be particularly adept in one area, for example complex numbers, but they will also be strong across the board.

High flyers are an important asset for the organization and will be persistent in requesting ongoing learning and development. Whilst they will be proactive, they should not be allowed to set the agenda or take up more than their fair share of resources. One usually effective approach once an individual is identified as having high potential is to set up a mentoring relationship with one of the business leaders. This mentor will hopefully provide a long-term supportive relationship in which they support the individual in broadening their understanding of the business, provide project opportunities that challenge and expose the individual and induct them into more senior relationships. They should also provide significant challenge as well a support so that the high-flying individual can develop their critical faculties further.

The role of mentor is a complex one which needs clarity and training in order to be carried out well. The role of mentor will be discussed later in the book.

Knowledge workers

Knowledge workers are those members of organizations whose specific value lies in their knowledge and skills. Typical examples include lawyers, accountants, marketing or HR professionals. They are expected to retain a body of knowledge and take an active part in ensuring their own development through continuing professional development. Some organizations will facilitate this learning through provision of in-house development opportunities. These employees are typically members of professional bodies, which give them their certificate to practice. Development for these employees is partly a tool to engage them with the organization and its goals as well as with their specific profession.

CASE STUDY

Leading to succeed at M&S

Lead to Succeed is Marks & Spencer's flagship leadership development programme, launched in 2009 and continues to run in partnership with leadership specialists Cirrus. The programme develops senior leaders to drive the business forward in a highly competitive marketplace.

The background

Marks & Spencer (M&S) is an international multi-channel retailer, operating in over 50 territories worldwide and employing almost 82,000 people. In 2009, M&S launched an ambitious transformation programme designed to deliver a step change in how the organization operated in response to the changing needs of customers and the challenges of the economic downturn. At the heart of the transformation were the M&S values of quality, value, service, innovation and trust.

The challenge

As part of the transformation programme, M&S wanted to build the capability of its senior leaders. The organization wanted to create fresh impetus and to galvanize its leaders to drive the business forward in the market. To achieve this, M&S decided to develop a challenging and innovative leadership development programme that would encourage collaborative working, a sharper focus on the customer and clearer accountability.

The solution

The resulting programme, called Lead to Succeed, is closely aligned to the organization's strategic objectives, and targets the development of the 350 most senior M&S employees. It is designed to provide challenging learning opportunities, to develop leadership capability, and to aid succession. The programme was launched in February 2009 and is still going strong today, as new leaders become part of the top 350.

As part of the programme, M&S defined its own 'leadership brand', drawing on the core attributes of effective leaders outlined in the book, *Head, Heart, and Guts: How the world's best companies develop complete leaders* by Dotlich *et al* (2006) The authors argue that 'whole' leaders combine head, heart, and guts – head to set strategy, heart to connect with the world, and guts to make instinctive and intuitive decisions based on clear values.

In addition, the M&S leadership brand has its own unique distinguishing attributes of driving innovation, achieving quality and building trust.

Programme outline

The programme consists of four modules and combines face-to-face learning, business simulations with professional role-players, feedback from pre-course assessments and buddy review. In preparation, participants complete a 360-degree assessment and profiling questionnaires. Ongoing coaching ensures that individuals define their own goals in line with the organization's strategic objectives and provides support to help individuals embed learning and achieve goals.

The first module helps participants understand the principles and advantages of great leadership to both the individual and the organization. It raises awareness of leadership styles and preferences and develops communication and influencing skills. In addition, participants develop strategies to encourage effective decision-making. By the end of the first module, each participant has created an individual leadership development plan, which they continue to build on and review throughout the programme.

The second module develops the understanding and skills to lead teams, manage team dynamics and drive team development. Participants learn how to increase collaboration within and between teams to drive organizational performance. This module also focuses on developing creativity and innovation in others, leading change, building relationships and coaching.

The third module helps participants to understand the organization as a dynamic system and to develop strategies to operate successfully in a complex, changing and competitive environment. They learn about organizational culture, the role leaders play, how they can influence the organization and how the organization can influence them. Central to this learning is a focus on customers and the need for participants to align themselves and their activities with business priorities.

The fourth and final module provides participants with opportunities to identify and review key learnings from the programme. Participants make a presentation to members of the M&S Executive Committee on business impact, which helps to demonstrate return on investment. Together, participants share experiences of successful learning implementation and celebrate the completion of the programme. Each individual participant leaves with a clear vision for his or her future focus as a leader.

The benefits

Lead to Succeed is considered a flagship programme by M&S and a key component in its people strategy. The programme has resulted in sustainable success. It has strengthened the capability of senior leaders to lead change. In addition, millions of pounds' worth of financial benefits have been identified as a result of the programme – a combination of increases in productivity, reduced external recruitment costs, and cost savings.

Significant behavioural change has been noted, and the organization has witnessed considerable change in the way that participants tackle challenges. Evaluation shows leaders embody the M&S leadership brand values and act as role models. The programme receives consistently high ratings from participants.

The programme brings together people from the commercial and operational areas of the business. The majority of delegates confirm that one of the greatest benefits is the creation of new and meaningful working relationships and connections across the organization.

The programme has focused the attention of leaders on what they specifically can do to move the business forward and to drive shareholder value. It encourages them to focus on their own accountabilities and that of their teams. The programme gives them a number of tools to support them in developing their teams to deliver high performance. The delegates also spend time focusing on leading change and supporting their teams through change; this has led to much more proactive thinking about change management and increasing levels of activity around change planning.

There are many opportunities during the programme for leaders to build the skills and confidence to challenge others in order to improve performance. For example, the final module of the programme gives participants the opportunity to give feedback to the board, and discuss what support they need to take their proposals forward. This has resulted in some robust, challenging and creative conversations about how things work now and how they need to work in the future. These types of conversations did not happen on a regular basis prior to the programme. This has supported a number of delegates to challenge more in the workplace, giving them the confidence and skills to do this more effectively. This has also encouraged leaders to take control of situations to ensure they get the outcomes they believe are right. Many participants have shared examples of situations where they have taken a different approach in a challenging situation, and explained this has resulted in a successful outcome.

Throughout the programme, delegates support each other's development through one-to-one buddy relationships. This enables them to build their skills and confidence as a coach through real-time practice. Many participants have continued these relationships after completing the programme.

Overall, this programme is a tremendously successful example of how changing leadership behaviour and building capability in line with organizational values and goals can lead to long-term, sustainable change.

In conclusion

This chapter has addressed the realities of learning. I have approached the technicalities of learning in some detail in order to demonstrate how learners really learn so that you are able to construct effective learning interventions. I have also considered the reality of organizational learning and the opportunities for the learning and development function to have an impact.

This will be expanded in Part Two of the book, which takes a more practical perspective to consider how you can build an effective learning and development function in your organization.

IN PRACTICE

How do you do it?

Introduction

The focus of this part of the book is entirely practical. Having explained the theory and described examples of the practical uses and applications of learning and development I intend to introduce a range of tools and techniques that you may be able to use for learning and development in your own setting. My aim here is to give you an overview of the potential activities and interventions involved in this area. I will consider all the stages that are typically encountered:

- *Identifying the need* – working out what needs to be developed, how each area should be prioritized and which areas are more amenable to development.

- *Making the case* – balancing all the various factors to put together a clear rationale for the interventions you believe to be in the best long-term interests of the organization.

- *Sourcing interventions* – once you have a clear idea of what it is you want to work on, where it is you are trying to get to and you have back up from the organization – exactly what will you do?

- *Follow-up* – monitoring the impact of the intervention as it progresses, adapting where necessary and following up with individuals and teams to ensure adequate transfer of learning and keeping senior management informed and supportive of the intervention.

- *Evaluation* – how do you know the interventions are working? A tricky but essential phase to quantify the impact of your interventions to demonstrate their effectiveness and garner ongoing management support for your other interventions.

However, first a couple of health checks; this is very much a simple introduction to a complex area. The activities identified above typically take place iteratively and simultaneously with multiple projects. That is, depending on your situation you could be working on every stage of the process for varying projects at any one time. For successful transfer of learning it also needs to be thoroughly integrated with the full range of people initiatives, including performance management, employee relations and talent management in particular.

You would be well advised to seek support in both your own skill development as well as the readiness of your organization before setting up formal learning and development processes. What the following chapters do is provide an initial outline and guide to the options available to you. You should identify which of these may be of use and follow them up in the extensive additional literature. Some may also require engaging additional support in the form of external consultancy.

Identifying the need

How to discern the underlying factors

So, you see a need for learning and development in your organization – but what precisely is it that needs developing and why? It is absolutely essential to carry out some form of structured analysis to ensure that you are aware of the full range of learning needs and can prioritize them. So often organizations jump into a development activity without sufficient consideration. Maybe a competitor is becoming more successful and their option seems good, or maybe a colleague has recommended the latest fad to your MD. Whatever the pressure to provide something, take some time to choose what you do carefully. The budget is inevitably limited and you will be required to demonstrate healthy returns, so take a structured approach to:

1 understanding the business situation, its drivers and how you can enhance organizational effectiveness through people development;

2 analysing the levels of competence, and areas for development using the full range of sources available to you;

3 involving people from all levels and parts of the organization, asking their perspective, getting them to check out what you have found so far, building a consensus on what needs developing – essentially, building an awareness of the needs;

4 formalizing your survey and discussions into presentations and agreement to act, with budget allocation and senior management support.

The sources of your information will be diverse, including the organizational strategy and vision, business results, professional reading, competitor benchmarking, views of directors and senior managers, feedback from customers and suppliers, etc – the sources of information concerning learning and development needs are almost endless. These needs also persist. They tend to be endemic within organizations in general, or specific to industry, nation or organization. This is why you are likely to find, for example, junior manager generic development interventions across the world of work. These are typically a combination of short courses with follow-up line manager and coaching sessions to ensure that the development has been 'fixed' or to put it technically, transferred to the workplace.

A key underlying factor, which grows and also changes in its detail and impact, is variation across employee groups. We have a tendency, usually for the sake of simplicity, to group employees together and provide unitary solutions for them, as described above in consideration of junior manager development. However, there is a broad range of individual differences ranging from motivators through to cultural norms that should be considered when investigating underlying learning needs.

In particular, there are differences in the ways of thinking and approaching problems that are characteristic of cultures or nationalities. We discussed one way of understanding international variations in Chapter 3 when we considered Hofstede's (1984) categories of international cultural differences. When working to identify learning and development needs these differences should be taken into account as they can have a profound impact on the functioning of a business.

CASE STUDY

A number of years ago I worked with an international drinks business that had a head office in the UK. The organization at that time had a number of sales and marketing-focused subsidiaries across the newly emerging region of Central and Eastern Europe. The culture in these areas was highly varied and in terms of learning needs was classified as primarily an issue of mutual understanding. However, one consistent issue was that a number of the countries had a significantly higher power distance than was typical in the UK, or that this organization perceived as desirable. The culture of the organization was typically task- and achievement-focused rather than hierarchically focused so that a purposeful, friendly and quite relaxed atmosphere pervaded the UK offices. Employees were usually assigned to a brand of drink and the development and support of this drink was their motivation and goal, not status. They typically appeared to feel free to approach more senior employees if they had concerns or ideas about their brand. They could be quite assertive with managers if they perceived a danger to their brand.

However, in one country in Eastern Europe in particular, the culture of high power distance meant that employees of a lower status were diffident with more senior members and did not sufficiently raise concerns or issues. This had an ongoing impact on penetration into the market so that the brand was not quite as successful in this country as in others. Clearly, there may have been a number of factors impacting this. However, the senior manager of this country was also an individual who had a preference for a more hierarchical approach. He was from the UK and this is an example of individual differences interacting with national cultural variations. He therefore encouraged a high power distance and separated a little from the head office in day-to-day work as he focused on building up the brands in that region. This in turn led to some isolation from the rest of the organization and informally within the organization he became known as 'the baron' ruling over a small feudal organization where he was the titular head. This allowed him to turn around sales in the short term to build a strong level of sales. However, it meant that the organization was not integrated, new schemes were not implemented, and sales-related activities such as merchandising were not properly put in place. The high power distance culture minimized the communication of real sales figures and the brand perception among customers was damaged. As a result, the long-term performance of both the brand and the organization as a whole in that region was badly damaged. It took a good five years, after the senior manager had been replaced, for it to recover to meet the levels of neighbouring countries.

When working in an international setting these cross-cultural differences impact organizational effectiveness in a number of ways. For example, specific national differences should be considered. Isenhour *et al* (2012) use Hofstede's (1984) cultural dimensions to criticize research on cultural variations between western and Chinese cultures. They indicate that it has been based on 'western theoretical models that do not always consider differences in culture and values... [and] many theories are underdeveloped because they fail to consider the critical role that cultural factors play in the management of employee behaviour'. This is partially due to the complexities of cultural variations, often studied at a national level but varying across country and localities. I worked with one junior manager in the UK whose pleasant manner, agreeableness, lack of assertiveness and consistent checking of her work had marked her out as inadequate and unable to progress. However, on closer investigation it became apparent that she had previously held a middle manager role in Sri Lanka, in a separate sector. She moved to the UK on marrying and joined this organization. However, the cultural differences were an unexpected shock to her and she found it very hard to adapt. Once her potential had been identified, a coaching intervention enabled her to conceptualize the differences, revealing them and by making them concrete in her mind, to then adjust to specific cultural variations and adapt to a more UK way of working.

These cultural differences apply both ways. Multinational corporations moving into the UK also need to adapt their approaches to local styles of developing people. For example, in the UK, employees will typically expect to be kept informed of the business goals and results as well as be given a clear induction process and regular ongoing development. This does not necessarily meet the expectations of organizations moving into the UK. It is interesting to question the extent to which national and organizational cultures influence one another. Certainly there is a trend towards homogeneity globally across cultures. This is driven in part by technological developments, eg when everyone has a fridge then shopping habits match the capacity of the fridge as well as local customs. This may also have a lot to do with the sales and marketing activities of global media corporations as well as other equally large but somewhat less-public corporations. Whether this will continue into the future is an interesting point to consider, and of interest here as it significantly impacts the potential effectiveness of learning and development interventions.

Learning needs emerging from cultural variation are particularly persistent and it may be that organizations need to consider their own structures and mission as well as learning and development (such as those countries with a higher power distance).

Using organizational information

There are two major categories to consider: group learning needs and individual learning needs. The major source of both of these in many instances is in fact the performance review cycle.

A perennial source of information about development needs is the performance management system. This process should be run in a systematic, organization-wide way that will ensure coverage of the whole organization in a manner that affects its values and business strategy. The effectiveness of the performance appraisal itself hinges on the understanding that employees have of the system and the coaching and interview skills of the line manager. Where the skills and understanding are in place, then the manager may be highly effective in drawing out key underlying areas for development. The line manager should be encouraged to additionally review the learning needs of their whole team in order to collate a generic map of the learning needs. This should be passed onto the next more senior manager who will be able to collate a broader perspective.

Every organization should undertake performance management. This consists of ongoing monitoring and development of employee performance. It reaches its peak in most organizations through the appraisal process. In the appraisal the employee and their direct line manager meet to discuss one-to-one the employee's performance over the last period, typically a year. They will typically consider the employee's achievement, particularly against their objectives, the way in which they work, for example through the use of competencies and additionally the short-term career plans and ongoing development needs of the employee. There are as many ways to structure and manage this process as there are organizations. However, the effectiveness of this process lies very much in the hands of the manager. The appraisal is a highly skilled activity and managers need both ongoing training to upskill them in developing their own capacity to appraise, as well as organizational support in communications and briefings for employees.

One of the major areas of conflict within a performance management system is in the dual purpose they often try to achieve, focusing on both quality of performance and also assigning reward for that performance. This conflicting purpose frequently means that employees feel compelled to put their best foot forward and rather than seeking support and advice for improving their performance, may be more likely to seek to change their manager's perspective on how good their performance has been. Similarly, the line manager is conflicted, wishing to motivate the employee, through various reward mechanisms such as development opportunities, job enrichment and pay. Simultaneously, they must conduct an incisive, accurate review of performance, most of which, for anyone, will not be perfect. An appraisal meeting without some negatives and areas for development has not got to the bottom of things and is far less worthwhile. This conflict between assessment for reward and assessment for development is more toxic than at first appears. It leads to misinformation throughout the organization as levels of performance are typically obfuscated in order to balance motivation, appropriate reward and development. This is exacerbated during economic downturns when the 'pot' at managers can dip into to reward employees may be highly constrained.

Many organizations adopt an annual appraisal process where everyone in the organization takes part in this formal review of their performance. Whilst this is by no means perfect, it is nonetheless a very good opportunity for HR to gather all of the development areas identified in order to build a more thorough picture of learning and development needs across the organization. The particular benefit is in its thorough nature. Where every employee has received an appraisal, then learning needs can be identified at a broad range of levels across the organization. For example, a manufacturing organization may look to see how learning needs are matched across various locations, or by function, say IT versus marketing. Geographical splits may also be useful and can be revealing about the quality of senior management in specific locations. It is essential to continue to keep in mind the importance of the quality of the appraisal in generating these learning needs. However, they do provide a thorough and very useful starting point for starting to plan interventions. Additionally, as they are identified across the organization over one time period, innovative, bespoke interventions can be designed on the basis of this information, and are also good value for money.

If this process is carried out consistently and systematically across the whole organization it can provide a robust, thoroughly evidenced identification of development needs. The benefit of this is that it provides a solid platform for identifying and planning interventions targeted specifically at clearly articulated areas of skill, knowledge, behaviour and attitude. This allows a corporate function such as a specialist L&D team to cross-match specific areas for development across the whole organization. This provides the opportunity to set up cross-organizational interventions. These have a range of benefits including cost benefit and encouraging interpersonal relations across diverse parts of the organization.

This forms the basis for planning to meet learning and development needs. The cyclical nature of the performance management system means that areas for development can be tracked over time, supporting evaluation of current interventions as well as spotting trends in areas for development needs and identifying clusters of repetitive areas for development, such as first line manager development. However, whilst the performance review provides a 'Rolls Royce approach' to the identification of learning and development needs, when conducted to a high standard, it is by no means the only approach to identification of learning needs.

Competencies in identifying learning needs

The use of competencies is a particularly useful form of analysis of learning needs as they are designed specifically for your organization. This is related to the performance management system as the competencies will typically be used as one measure of performance during the appraisal itself. Competencies are clusters of behaviours that describe how a specific job should be carried out. Whereas objectives identify what the employee should be required to achieve, competencies identify how the employee should carry out their role. For example, a frequent competence identifies planning and organization as a core behaviour. This indicates that employees should achieve their objectives through planning and organizing their work. For example, highly ambitious and aggressive young graduates may well over-achieve on objectives. However, if in doing so they upset a large proportion of the people they work with, then their performance is unacceptable, no matter how much they achieved. This is because sustainable achievement is essential and no one is likely to want to work with them in the future. The competence for planning and organizing is likely to include a number of elements around communicating their plans and agreeing schedules, meetings and allocation of work. Where they pay attention simply to this element in the way that they work, there is likely to be a significant rise in performance levels. This is before any of the other competencies are even considered. Although, clearly in practice an individual is assessed on every competence and similarly the organization will provide some form of development for each of these competencies.

Balanced scorecard

A balanced scorecard is a monitoring tool used by organizations that enables them to identify the core metrics for success. It was introduced by Kaplan and Norton in 1996 and usually identifies four perspectives from which to view the organization. These are typically:

1 *financial* – eg the average number of days it takes customers to pay, cash-flow metrics, wages, etc;

2 *the customer*;

3 *internal business process*;

4 *learning and development and innovation*.

Each of these is usually laid out in a two-by-two diagram, which is filled with targets. Based on the understanding that people tend to do what they are measured on, this may include such detailed elements as number of customer complaints, market share, waste targets, revenue and cost targets. It also specifies the learning and development needed to achieve the business goals. This may include innovation of new products or processes or new routes to market. For example, our case study organization Synch Ltd who you will come across shortly is a retailer of refurbished consumer IT goods, such as mobile phones, laptops, cameras, etc. They may identify YouTube clips demonstrating their products as a new route to contact potential customers. However, using YouTube for this purpose is complex and skilled. Therefore the learning and innovation target will identify both the innovative route to market and also the people development required to successfully build such a route.

This approach allows business leaders to focus the effort of the organization on specific activities and also measure success against the targets. It also provides an opportunity to understand the gaps, or learning needs where targets have not been met. This may be due to resource issues, such as not enough employees or insufficient time but may also indicate capability issues. This provides a platform for the learning and development professional to investigate the cause of the gap and if appropriate put in place an intervention to enable the organization to achieve its targets in the future. In this way learning and development can be closely aligned to organizational growth and can add identifiable value.

The balanced scorecard, like any report card, should be a living document and will typically be updated on a regular basis. Depending on the organization this may be quarterly or annually. It will also be cascaded and adapted throughout the organization, ensuring that objectives are precise and appropriate to local units as well as aligned across the organization. The benefit of this for learning and development is that interventions linked to the scorecard will also be precise and focused on exactly what the organization needs to learn in order to achieve the current targets. The difficulties with this are that whilst funding tends to flow for targets on the scorecard, for other, perhaps more nebulous, but no less important needs, such as developing potential for future succession or mid- to senior managers, funding is restricted. That is, what is measured is acted upon; what is not measured may well be ignored. This is usually not to the long-term benefit of the organization as it can hinder its adaptability to new economic circumstances.

Competitor analysis

One particularly effective approach to identifying learning and development needs is through benchmarking. This approach became popular in the 1990s and is still used today in adapted forms. It essentially identifies key competitors and uncovers the processes they use in order to identify best practice. For example, Amazon has a strong capability in technology development, with its ability to identify potential purchases based on customer history as well as its one-click buying technology. This is especially relevant to competitors such as eBay, Waterstones and Barnes & Noble. The role of HRD here is to identify the skills, knowledge and attitudes required in employees in order to be able to not copy the outcome but rather use an understanding of the business processes to adopt best practice and so outcompete their rivals. Thus, the identification of learning needs emerges from detailing the core business processes and identifying what skills, knowledge and capabilities employees need to be able to carry out those practices and processes to the highest standard. This analysis is an ongoing process that aims to retain competitiveness in a rapidly changing marketplace.

Industry standards

The importance of industry standards to learning and development varies primarily by sector and industry. Some industries, usually due to the impact of poor performance, are more highly regulated in terms of, for example, continuing professional development. The learning and development approach in these cases needs to be structured around the regulatory requirements first. Note that solicitors have a strict code of development focusing on continuous updating of their knowledge concerning developments in the law as well as skill elements concerning, for example, practice management. This is developed as continuing professional development (CPD), which is prescribed within certain parameters. For example, using years of post-qualification experience (PQE) a solicitor must attend certain modules on practice management, including a solid understanding of the financial elements of running a practice as well as holding money for clients in client accounts.

There is usually a plethora of organizations that can support learning and development in cost-effective and focused ways. For instance, large suppliers to law firms often put on marketing events which include some element of legal update and can be incorporated as part of an individual solicitor's requirement for CPD points. There are also online courses, which can be paid for via annual licence or pay-per-click, as well as provision by the solicitors' regulatory authority themselves.

I have used solicitors as an example because, like other professionals such as medics their work has an immediate impact on clients and so their ongoing development is closely regulated. However, every profession and career has a significant ongoing requirement for learning which should be attended to, whether it is a regulatory requirement or not.

CASE STUDY

Synch Ltd

Synch Ltd is a privately-owned and owner-managed retailer of refurbished personal IT items such as mobile phones, laptops, tablets, cameras, etc. It also provides a thriving repair service which gives the opportunity to build customer relationships for repeat business. Synch owns 20 stores across the south and south-west of the UK, focusing on town centres in market towns such as Trowbridge and Witney. These tend to have a high proportion of retired and low-income families.

Their primary customer groups are 'silver surfers', families on single incomes or mid-to-low pay and finally students who need price-sensitive technology for their studies. Each of these groups has a desired price point of between 30–50 per cent of usual retail process. However, in other ways they are quite a diverse group. For example, students frequently know as much if not more than the sales assistant and will make a fairly rapid purchase with little support. However, they are less likely to return for either support or a repeat purchase, except consumables such as paper and ink, which have a low margin as the local out-of-town superstore provides them at a lower rate which Synch cannot compete with.

On the other hand, silver surfers are typically new to buying technology, but wish to buy a new piece of technology for a specific purpose, for example to use Skype to keep in touch with family members who are working abroad. The understanding of the technology is very diverse among this group, but they typically require a lot of support in setting up and using their purchase. They also frequently require ongoing support, but are very likely to be repeat purchasers over a longer period.

Synch source their merchandise from a broad range of sources. The most publicly communicated is through purchase and refurbishment of second-hand IT items. However, this provides only approximately 17 per cent of their merchandise. They purchase the majority of their stock directly from suppliers in Taiwan, Korea and Mainland China.

You are the HR manager for Synch, and being new to the role have spent the past few weeks travelling around the stores getting to know the various people and business situations. The primary issues you have identified include:

- Customer service quality is patchy with frequent examples of both outstanding and poor customer service. For example, on serving a customer with hearing difficulties one staff member was observed to shout instructions at him.

- Employee turnover is a little higher than you would have expected.

- Reward packages are set broadly at corporate levels, but store managers have a lot of discretion around bonus payments, commission and overtime.

- The performance management process is fairly consistent across the organization, but does not extend to the chief executive officer, or his first reports.

- The stock and stock levels vary between stores with some variance matching it in terms of employee skills in IT.

- Each store seems to operate as its own fiefdom with less of a corporate culture.

- This has led to some issues of lack of coordination across the organization, for example, with multiple supplies for repeat items such as shelving in the shops.

You also have access to a summary of the learning needs identified over the past two years, which were put together by your predecessor. You found them in a drawer as you were clearing a space for your folders. They have not been referred to by the owner or any other member of the management team.

Learning needs identified from performance management process:

- customer service skills, particularly among customer service assistants with zero-to-two years' service;

- updating specific IT/technology skills and understanding in customer service assistants with eight or more years' service;

- business awareness for assistant store managers;

- finance and management accounting for store managers;

- understanding of what other stores are doing;

- procurement skills;

- merchandising and store management for assistant store managers;

- people management skills for store managers.

Making the case

Once you have identified the organization's learning needs, you must prepare a case in order to access resources of some type to fill the gap that you have identified. The first thing to do is consider the evidence that you have gathered of the range of areas of learning and development and start to prioritize them. This is an activity that should be team-based. One of the primary difficulties for learning and development is the political nature of implementation that frequently emerges. In some organizations learning and development is seen as a punishment meted out to those who have not met targets. In many organizations, it is sought as a form of reward, with line managers occasionally promising attendance in return for support on some other project. To negotiate these rapids within your own organization you should consult with as wide a group of colleagues as possible in order to build a broad group consensus on specifically what these learning needs are, how filling them would support the business, and also, what could happen if they are not filled.

When you are considering the relative priorities of learning and development, it is essential that you consider them in the light of the organization's mission, vision and values, alongside the current competitive realities. In order to fill the learning and development gap that you have identified you will need to access resources. Therefore you need to build a compelling case for meeting these needs. Alongside the organization's ethos, you should consider the environment in which it operates, both external and internal:

- What are the drivers of change in the far environment? How are they likely to develop over the next 5–10 years? How can your organization respond to them?

- What is happening in your near competitor environment? Do you have a new competitor? How are customers behaving? Can you predict changes in the competitiveness of your industry? How will the typical price point change? Are suppliers becoming more concentrated?

- How effective and efficient is your internal environment? What are your primary resources and capabilities? How can the learning and development function maximize the capabilities of the organization?

One useful tool for identifying the competitive reality of your organization is a PESTLE analysis. This analysis considers the far business environment; that is those external changes that the organization must respond to, but probably is less able to influence. The 2009 recession is a prime example of such an external factor – organizations that did not respond quickly by cutting costs and adapting their business model, could find themselves in difficulties later. The PESTLE model identifies specific segments of the external environment. It is a framework for identification of the macro-economic drivers and analysis of that environment based on the work of Fahey and Narayanan (1986):

- *Political* – What is the impact of local and national political initiatives, for example, increased funding for apprentices? What is the political milieu, for example is the government tending towards restriction and cost-cutting, or are they building resources? What is the regulator environment like?

- *Economic* – What is the balance between demand and supply of goods? Are prices tending to rise, stay stable or fall? What is the state of the national/international economy? How does that impact the levels of confidence in the economy?

- *Sociological* – What are the current and emerging trends across society? For example, is there a strong trend towards green issues, health and environmental conservation?

- *Technological* – What are the drivers of technology? Is there a push towards certain types of technology, eg miniaturization through electronic engineering, or the use of new materials?

- *Legal* – What changes are there in the legislative environment? For example in terms of employment law, immigration, pension age, etc.

- *Environmental* – What are the drivers for environmental issues, for example, what are the current recycling and conservation norms?

When working through the PESTLE model, it is important to focus not just on what has happened, but also what is predicted to happen over the next few years. Particularly with learning and development, you are supporting the organization to meet emerging and not historical challenges. Therefore, it is crucial to put time into considering the ways that the organization will have to develop in order to meet new challenges. You may find that there is some research already conducted and available to you, so it may be helpful to conduct some form of desk research. You should also meet with senior managers and business leaders to seek their perspective. Even where there is considerable information, are they clear that this is still accurate, or has the picture shifted? Clearly, this is not an exact science and there are many unpredicted surprises awaiting us in the future, but preparation and a careful consideration of what is emerging will be a considerable help in meeting those challenges.

This is an area in which you may benefit from discussion of this topic with others across your organization. Each colleague is likely to have some useful input based on his or her experience, observations and specific expertise. By selecting colleagues to discuss this with, you will be able to generate a thorough picture of the current and emerging drivers in the far external environment. These colleagues will also be more likely to support you in making a case for the intervention to fill the development need you have identified. As well as discussing this with colleagues, there is also a large amount of information accessible; depending on the industry that you work in, there may be information available in the industry literature. You may be able to access this through a range of means, including your own organization, for example the marketing function, an internet search, industry bodies, etc. However, it is always useful to add to a generic PESTLE both to build support in the business and to bring it fully up to date and bespoke for your own organization.

Once you have identified the drivers in your far external environment, you could consider an analysis of your near, competitive environment. This environment is closer to your own and involves those organizations and individuals with whom you interact regularly such as competitors, customers and suppliers. A very useful model for analysing the near environment is Porter's five forces model (1979).

What are the implications of these external forces on Synch? Do you agree that industry rivalry is only moderate? What other factors do you consider to be relevant for them? Given this information, what do you think are the primary learning and development priorities?

Porter's 'five forces' is a standard model for understanding the degree of competitiveness in a specific industry. It is especially useful for building a mental map, or schema, of the competitive dynamics of the industry. As a business-focused HR professional this is an important element of the role. Consequently, it will be a valuable exercise for a generalist to undertake in order to ensure that they are aware of the dynamics and sensitivities of the industry as a whole and the potential impacts on their organization. Its additional value for learning and development is in the predictability that it garners for developing bespoke, industry-specific interventions that enable employees to be sensitive to the impact of changing industry climates. For example, negotiating skills workshops for the purchasing function may benefit from a predictive sensitivity that enables them to fully appreciate the industry dynamics, and so get a better price.

Finally, in terms of appreciating the impact of the external environment and predicting the specific skills, knowledge and ability that you are developing for, a review of the internal environment completes the picture. This can be considered in terms of the resources and capabilities contained within the organization. Resources are those assets, human, fixed and intangible that

FIGURE 5.1 Porter's five forces model (applied Synch Limited)

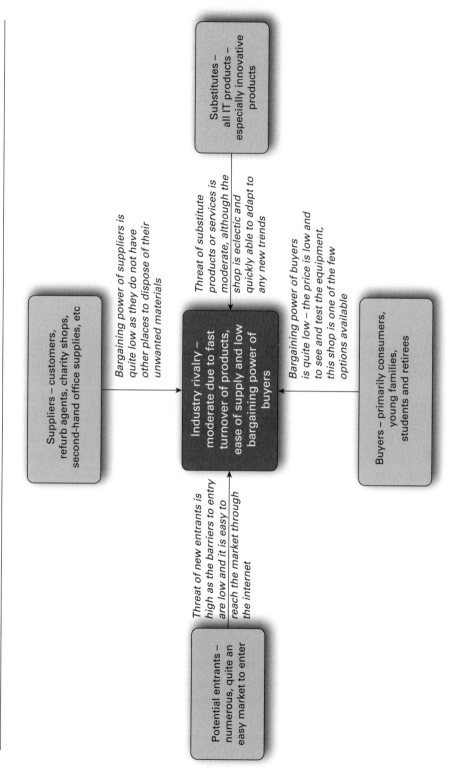

the organization owns or controls. For example, an organization such as an insurance company may be considered to have tangible resources such as financial assets, a property portfolio, office furniture, car fleet, etc. It may also possess intangible assets such as the actual process for identifying risk and assigning an insurance rate to that risk; brand recognition assets, intellectual property of the databanks built up on customers and human capital assets in the people it employs. Capabilities are the specific abilities of the firm to combine these assets in order to provide value. For example, this particular insurance company may have the capacity to respond very rapidly to new business or to manage the portfolio of insurance products to maximize revenue or market share or net profit. This is one way of understanding how the organization builds value. It applies equally to private, public and third sector organizations as it focuses on building value at a number of levels. For example, a hospital may build value in the community through enhanced levels of health whilst a school may build value through increased levels of skill and knowledge.

This analysis of the fit between external and internal environments is often conducted as a SWOT analysis. This form of analysis considers the strengths and weaknesses of the organization, ie its current and potential resources and capabilities, against the threats and opportunities of the environment. The degree to which there is a mismatch indicates a potential for areas for learning and development. The decision on how to manage the mismatch is a strategic company-wide decision that the HR function should be fully involved in. It is the results of this discussion in particular that should confirm the specific areas for learning and development that are priorities within the organization.

Having done this analysis you will benefit in three particular ways:

1 Your reputation as a business-focused, future-facing HR business partner should be enhanced.

2 The case for learning and development interventions will be clear, enabling a clear case for resources to meet those needs to be made.

3 There will be a shared understanding of the strategic direction and need for development among the managers you interviewed and those they discussed it with. Given the right conditions (ie no emergencies to distract them) you will have started to create a desire for further development from within the business itself.

It is very important to seek the championing of a learning and development intervention by a senior manager or director. This individual will be able to support the case when you are absent and provide further support if the implementation of the learning and development intervention is not entirely smooth. This is generally the case! They can also be called upon to influence across the organization to ensure that all parts of the organization understand the imperative for the intervention.

One valuable tool for making the case for learning and development is the negative argument of what will happen if the training and development is not carried out. If you have done your research well and it is backed up by evidence, then it should be very clear that the learning gaps exist and need to be filled. By exploring what would happen if they were not filled, you give senior managers a powerful tool to evaluate their options for resourcing projects. For example, in a mid-sized telecommunications organization, project management may have been identified as an area of weakness. A consideration of the costs of poor project management will be evocative for senior managers. The primary costs may include:

- stiff financial penalties for not achieving service level agreements;
- loss of brand value through poor customer service;
- opportunity opened for competitors to steal work from under your nose.

This approach highlights the value of the declared cost of learning and development against the potential costs of poor employee performance. This brings us to the importance of evaluating learning and development interventions.

It is both a professional requirement but also a sensible protective mechanism to consistently demonstrate the value of your work, through ongoing evaluation and constant improvement. If you are lucky enough to be in a situation where there has been some evaluation, then you will have a basis on which to make a case for the intervention that you are seeking to introduce. However, should you be in a position where you would like to introduce a wholly new intervention or do not have any evaluative information to hand, then it will be harder work to build a case. From the perspective of senior managers, costs are constrained and so any expenditure must be thoroughly examined for both the financial layout and also the opportunity cost. This cost involves what else could have been done with the resources that are being spent on one intervention.

The cost of learning and development interventions may also be considered part of the total reward package for employees. Total reward is a concept that incorporates both financial reward, such as basic pay, commission, share options, etc with non-financial reward. These may include benefits such as dental or private medical health, holiday, membership of clubs at cut prices as well as learning and development opportunities, etc. These elements are all valued and the value of the total package is communicated to employees. Ideally, this communication indicates to employees the value of every element.

Organizational readiness

Organizations vary in the degree of acceptability of learning and development, or their readiness to receive it. This is related primarily to the organizational culture. For example, in a 'blame' culture where most employees are fearful of 'being found out', learning and development is generally seen as a punishment and so fought against. However, in a high-performing organization, capability is seen as key so, in general, anything that supports enhanced capability, such as learning and development, is welcomed.

Preskill *et al* (1999) define organizational readiness in six dimensions: culture; leadership; systems and structures; communication; teams; evaluation. These dimensions identify the gold standard or readiness to be a learning organization. However, they are useful as a high standard to consider the general degree of organizational readiness.

Culture

This includes elements of mutual respect and co-operation between employees, a focus on constant improvement, discussion of issues and frequent opportunities to reflect on work. Mistakes are seen as positive opportunities to learn and so employees are willing to take appropriate risks, for example, trying out a new form of employee communication. Employees are encouraged to become involved in decision-making and are typically consulted by managers.

Leadership

Managers take a coaching role and facilitate employee learning. They are open to negative feedback and focus on serving the organization rather than gathering power and prestige. They encourage the sharing of knowledge and skills among employees and model the importance of learning.

Systems and structures

The work environment is open and accessible with a minimum of red tape and ease of communication and relationship between departments and functions. The performance management scheme rewards learning and development as well as supporting the learning of others. Employees are clear about how their learning contributes to the broader organizational mission.

Communication

Communication is readily available and feedback is sought to understand performance levels. New information is disseminated quickly so that everyone has the information needed to make decisions related to their jobs.

Teams

The organization is structured into teams that are supported to resolve conflict, share learning, and provide a supportive and encouraging environment to achieve goals.

Evaluation

An understanding of how we are doing is built into everyday work as performance levels are not taken for granted. There is a focus on systematic inquiry to ensure that any changes are working effectively and that work is optimized.

Approach client group as a key account management group

There is a great deal of literature on key account management. It is usually reserved for those who consult to or sell large complex projects to clients in other companies. However, as a learning and development professional you will be acting as an internal consultant and many of the approaches used as part of key account management will form a useful part of your toolkit.

The essence of key account management is in its long-term approach to building strong relationships with client groups. This allows for an in-depth understanding of the client groups and high levels of trust between both parties. If you work from a corporate head office base then this approach will allow you to properly understand your client group. It will also encourage your client group to contact you sooner rather than later to discuss emerging issues. This enables you to provide solutions in good time, when they may be trialled and implemented carefully rather than as a reaction to clear problems. The skills you will need in order to build credibility and trust within your client group include financial, consultative, planning, interpersonal and influencing skills.

As an internal consultant you benefit from being available and cost-free to your client group (relatively) compared to external consultants. However, you may find that as you are internal to the organization they do not feel entirely free to discuss the situation with you and you will need to work hard to gain their trust. On the other hand you do have a strong in-depth understanding of the business, which means that you can quickly understand their issues. This enables you to balance competing interests quickly and consider the full range of stakeholders, influencing factors, long-term impacts, etc.

Cockman *et al* (1992) identify the main stages of internal consultancy as:

1 *Gaining entry* – building your reputation within the client group and demonstrating your capability.

2 *Contracting* – this essential phase is often glossed over but is a very important part of the process. What exactly is required and what can you offer? When will the project be completed? Objectives should be explicitly agreed. You should take care to explore how this need has emerged and work to uncover the unspoken expectations at this point.

3 *Collecting data* – find out what the real issue is, perhaps by discussing it with people through interviews or focus groups, perhaps by observing or perhaps by trying it yourself!

4 *Diagnosing* – this is the crux of the project. Having worked out what is really going on, what do you suggest the team do about it? What are the underlying development needs that must be addressed?

5 *Generating options* – closely related to diagnosing. What is the range of activities that can be undertaken to address the issue?

6 *Implementing/taking action* – The issue remains in the ownership of the team, so whilst you may support taking action, perhaps running the interventions, the final decisions remain with the contracting manager.

7 *Disengaging* – once you have been able to provide at least a partial solution, you must retire from this project. If you do not, there is a risk that the project will be undermined as you take on ownership. Also, the organization will have other areas where you could add further value.

Sourcing interventions

Once an analysis of learning needs has been completed it is essential to follow up with some form of intervention, which needs to be clearly communicated to the organization. The reason for this is that frequently the research piece will involve the support of a broad range of employees and managers. They have given their time and support and so should be acknowledged and should see the fruits of their labour. If this does not happen, then cynicism and a diminishing of respect for the HR and HRD functions will creep in. It is similar to survey fatigue where employees can be particularly negative when they repeatedly complete opinion surveys but there are no apparent changes to the organization.

There is a broad range of interventions that may be carried out. This is also an area in which fashions dominate, with one area being considered significantly more 'hot' than another – an element which may play into the hands of senior managers but of which you should remain cautious – not all movement is growth! There are a number of dimensions along which training interventions can vary.

Universal or specific

The learning needs that you have identified may relate to one specific group of employees, or they may relate to broad populations, perhaps even the whole organization. You may have identified a broad-based area for development, usually relating to either legislative changes or fast-moving competitors. An example of this that I have experienced is the move towards total quality that involves the whole organization in focusing on various business processes to ensure that they are good as they can be and seeking constant improvement. This universal approach is a form of organization development in which cross-functional small project groups closely investigate business processes, such as customer billing or the performance management system. They take a fresh, disinterested view of the process to find ways to improve it to be the best it can. Popular in the 1990s, this approach continues across a range of organizations and involves small project groups seeking to ensure that each and every process is maximized. Interventions may also be specific, for example ensuring that customers are welcomed with the first few minutes of entry to a store.

Is there a qualification to be awarded?

If there is a qualification, that will both determine at least some of the content of your intervention and may also raise its status in the eyes of participants. However, it is important to at least 'personalize' the intervention so that it provides extra value for the organization. This may include organization-specific routines and ways of bedding in the learning. It may also include onwards development routes that are specific to the organization. If there is not a recognized qualification it may be possible to gain recognition for the training through the ERP (employer recognition framework) and QCF (Qualifications and Credit Framework). Somewhat complex and bureaucratic, the QCF is a framework adopted at a national level by the Qualification and Curriculum Authority (QCA). It could allow you to design your intervention to suit your own organization and then in consultation with the QCA, adapt it to enable employees to gain recognized qualifications to support their career development. This is likely to enhance a number of areas within HR, including your employer brand and employee engagement.

Mode of delivery

Learning and development interventions may be delivered in a broad range of ways, including face-to-face, e-learning, small local group, off-site training course, one specific intervention, etc. They may be more or less acceptable to your organization. For example, if the culture is so hardworking and macho that people strive to demonstrate that they cannot be away from their jobs, even for a couple of hours – then e-learning will be severely compromised and you would be better to encourage them to attend a more traditional training event off-site. A number of these ways will be discussed in detail in the next chapter.

Employee led versus externally directed

Learning and development interventions may be directed at so many different levels, skills, behaviours that the leadership of the intervention may, at times, be more appropriately held by internal employees rather than 'experts'. This can be the case when undertaking more personal learning and coaching is potentially useful. For example, during a merger, employees from each organization may be nominated to explain the culture and processes of their own side of the organization as a way of starting to properly understand each other and so build stronger working relationships. Or, during initial graduate development it can be useful to have a graduate from the previous year share their experiences and give advice on how best to get on in the new organization. One benefit of internally led development interventions is the development and profile that it gives the individual leading the intervention.

Externally directed development is appropriate for:

- areas that are new to the organization;
- skills that the organization does not hold in-house;
- senior and top manager development where issues of status may hold individuals back;
- where it is more cost-effective to source development externally;
- where mixing with delegates from other organizations will support the individuals' learning.

Sourced externally, in-house or a mix of the two

When contracting external providers there are a number of important points to address:

- *Internally* – As far as possible internal provision tends to be the preferred option, especially in larger organizations. Therefore, when you are using up a development budget on external provision there are a number of important questions to ask. It may simply be a need for external expertise that you do not have in-house. However, given the realities of organizational politics there may also be other reasons for hiring external provision.

  Questions you should ask include: What is the expressed and covert reason for contracting external provision? The expressed reason will concern the development needs. This may well be the whole reason for contracting external providers. However, it is always worth taking a second look – are there additional reasons why external providers are required? Often it is so that there will be someone to blame if the intervention is not evaluated as effective.

- *Supplier* – There are a broad range of suppliers who could potentially meet your needs. However, everything you initially find out about them will be part of their sales – even if it is a conference speech. It is therefore important to investigate them and their expertise as closely as possible.

  Questions you should ask include: How have you heard of them? Are they recommended by a trusted third party? Have they been validated by the appropriate professional body? What can they offer by way of demonstrating their effectiveness, for example, testimonials, client list, case studies? Is there an opportunity for you to observe them in action and meet with other clients? Have they worked in organizations similar to your own? Do they understand the way your industry works? What happens to any intellectual property you jointly develop? Will your primary contact be the person you worked with during the sales process? Are all their employees trained to a high standard?

- *Objectives* – You should have a clear idea of what your organization needs to achieve. However, it is useful to clarify these and agree them in writing.

    Questions you should ask include: What exactly is it you want? What are the specific learning objectives as well as the desired impact on the organization? What are your parameters in terms of time, budget, people to support internally, etc? What degree of upskilling in-house would you prefer? Sometimes external providers will upskill internal employees at cost – this is useful if there is likely to be a repeat of the business, or you may take those skills in-house at a later date.

Given all of these questions and caveats, when seeking an external provider of learning and development interventions:

1 Be certain of all the answers to the questions above – in particular, your objectives, budget, acceptable methods and any specific limiting factors, eg in some organizations you must/may not use offices/training facilities, etc.
2 Contact the appropriate professional body for a list of providers.
3 Ask around your organization and professional network for recommendations.
4 Do a Google search for the areas you are interested in – see the broad range of what is available.
5 Do some 'fishing' – phone some of the providers for an initial 'chat'.
6 Meet with the providers who are of particular interest to you; look them up on the companies house website if they are a limited liability company. Remember, while they may be experts in their arena, your specific learning need is not generic. How sensitive do you think they will be to your organizational culture? To what extent can they adapt their programme to best meet your organizational goals in this learning need? Do you have a 'niggle' you can't specify? Listen to this and discuss it with colleagues to see if it is perhaps simply an interpersonal issue, or an 'early-warning signal' of potential difficulties. Do you think the potential providers will persist in sales mode once you have engaged them, or can you trust that they do have your organization's best interests at heart?

7 Once you are certain that one of the providers will be able to fulfil the brief, work with senior managers to set up a 'beauty parade'. This is a substantial session where potential providers are asked to make a pitch for your business, ideally two to four potential providers. The benefits of this are that it enables you to easily compare them, they will be likely to respond to the seriousness of your invitation by putting their best foot forward, perhaps offering incentives and also providing a very clear working proposal.

8 Agree with senior managers on your preferred supplier and a final sense check of this as an agreed approach.

9 Now, you can contract with your preferred supplier. Make sure that the contract is watertight from your perspective; consider overt costs, intellectual property rights – do they belong to you or the provider? What have you agreed about the degree of upskilling of in-house employees? What are the precise service level agreements? What follow-up support will be available? How will the intervention be evaluated?

At this point you should now have a clear programme organized to meet your specific learning need. You should work to build up a high degree of trust between yourself and the providers, whilst monitoring their inter-actions with the wider organization. Evaluation of the intervention should begin almost immediately. Particularly for the first few interventions, there should be close evaluation to manage any teething problems. This will help ensure that the programme runs smoothly and also prevent any serious mishaps, which can rapidly cause a programme to fall into disrepute in the organization. This is particularly important for the ongoing success of the programme, as participants are essentially present due to the goodwill of their own managers. If the programme gains a poor reputation then participant numbers will begin to drop and the programme may not recover.

You should try to ensure that the first few sessions are successful and that any teething troubles are quickly ironed out. Then, communicate the success of the programme to the appropriate people. This may include e-mails detail-ing events to the sponsoring senior managers as well as putting a piece on the organizational intranet or in the newsletter.

Follow-up

At the same time, consider the extent to which the learning is transferring to the workplace. You should devise an approach to ensure that the learning is measured and find ways to ensure that it 'sticks'. These may include briefing line managers on what has taken place, making it part of the employees' objectives to demonstrate use of the learning or coaching to support transfer of the learning. This element is typically left until it is too late, once training has been evaluated 6 to 12 months later. It is better to be proactive and find a way to ensure that learning is used to benefit the organization early on. The precise way that this is done depends on a wide range of factors, including the activity levels of the HRD function! However, it should be made a priority to optimize the success of the intervention.

Evaluation

Evaluation of learning and development is a core activity that is central to effective management of the function. Every other function is subject to measurement through both direct and indirect means. For the learning and development function to be an accepted part of the broader business team it is important that it is subject to the same levels of scrutiny as other parts of the business. These will include measurement of the functioning of the department itself, for example, measurement of delivery of key performance indicators against budget, employee satisfaction levels, employee retention levels, sickness days, etc. In addition, the programmes and interventions that the function delivers should also be evaluated. This will enable an assessment of their value to both the individual and the business. For learning and development this is particularly complex due primarily to the difficulty in measuring the performance of people going about their daily roles. To then be able to directly compare performance before and after a learning intervention is almost impossible, for a range of reasons that have been discussed in this chapter.

The evaluation of learning and development interventions will be covered in more detail in Chapter 7. It essentially involves ensuring that the intervention is fit for purpose, that it enables learners to enhance their skills, knowledge and attitudes/behaviours and finally that it delivers sufficient value for the organization. The number of factors is such that it is very difficult to optimize learning and development interventions. Each facilitator is likely to seek to optimize their intervention, but if they move on, so much of the input will have been processual knowledge that a replacement facilitator will need to start to build the programme up again themself.

DIAGNOSTIC QUESTIONNAIRES

These questionnaires have been designed to support you in your analysis of the learning need, its underlying factors and potential remedies. They are designed to cover a broad range of situations. You may find only a small part of them of use. Feel free to adapt them to your own circumstances as is useful.

Identifying the need

This questionnaire supports you in diagnosing the underlying learning need.

1 *What is the business situation?* Can you describe what has changed to bring about this learning need? What difference will it make when this need is met? Exactly how will the business benefit?

2 *Who is promoting this business need?* What evidence do they have? Do others agree with them?

3 *How does the evidence available complement the understanding of this need?* Is it performance management data? Operational data? Faults data? Feedback from others? How good is the information? What else would you like to know?

4 *What further information do you need to clarify the nature of this need?* How will you go about collecting this information?

5 *How does this need fit with your organizational definitions?* Does it fit into your competencies? What level is it? Is it a skill, knowledge, attitude or behavioural area?

6 *Who else should be involved in identifying this need?* How do they suggest the need may be met?

7 *Carry out an investigation of ways of meeting the need.* What are your initial findings?

8 *How will you communicate the need and potential intervention?*

9 *Who do you need to influence?* Who could help you in influencing?

10 *What is your end goal in identifying and meeting this need?* How will you know when it has been met?

Identification of stakeholders involved in the learning and development

This questionnaire supports you in identifying who should be involved in both identifying the need and in deciding on the appropriate intervention.

1 *List all those who have a specific interest in this learning need, their interest and influence.*

TABLE 5.1 Stakeholders who could influence the learning and development agenda

Name and position	Interest – input to understanding and meeting the learning need	Degree of influence 1 = high, 5 = low
1		
2		
3		
4		
5		
6		
7		
8		
9		
10		
11		

TABLE 5.1 *continued*

Name and position	Interest – input to understanding and meeting the learning need	Degree of influence 1 = high, 5 = low
12		
13		
14		
15		
16		
17		
18		
19		
20		

2 *Are any of these people key?* Do they have particular interest or significance for this learning need?

3 *Do any of these people represent groups of interest?* For example employees, the organizational perspective, etc.

4 *Compare the perspectives and interests of these individuals or groups.* Are there any common themes? Do they inform either your understanding of the need, or how to meet the need?

Organizational readiness

This questionnaire aims to enable you to consider the readiness of the organization to receive and make full use of the chosen intervention.

1   Tick the appropriate box: 1 = very much, 2 = a great deal,
    3 = somewhat, 4 = not so much, 5 = almost never.

TABLE 5.2   Organizational readiness for learning and
                 development

	1	2	3	4	5
Is the organization used to ongoing learning and development?	1	2	3	4	5
Are people used to a range of learning and development interventions?	1	2	3	4	5
Are people willing to take responsibility for their own learning?	1	2	3	4	5
When undertaking development are people typically allowed to take time from their primary roles?	1	2	3	4	5
Is development seen as a punishment?	1	2	3	4	5
Do the top managers model development activities?	1	2	3	4	5
Is development focused solely on job-related skills?	1	2	3	4	5
Are there coaching or mentoring programmes available?	1	2	3	4	5
Do people actively follow up on the development identified in their performance reviews?	1	2	3	4	5
Are learning opportunities oversubscribed?	1	2	3	4	5

2   Review the answers you have given.

3   Consider the extent to which the organization can
    welcome and fully utilize the intervention you would
    like to suggest.

4   How can you enhance organizational readiness?

Planning and action

Introduction

This chapter takes a wholly practical approach to consider how to plan for learning and development and how to manage it. It considers the practical responsibilities for learning and development within an organization. It also concentrates on some specific areas of learning and development. My aim here is to enable you to start planning and then to deliver a high-quality and effective learning and development intervention.

The areas covered are:

- *Roles and responsibilities* – When deciding what needs you are going to address, it is essential to consider who has responsibility for what. What should the line manager do? The HR advisor? The chief executive and other board members have roles to play as well as the L&D practitioner. Each one has a key, specific role to be carried out. These roles and their value will be discussed below.

- *Identifying learning and development needs* – How do you know what to address? Carry out an investigation to identify skills, knowledge or ability gaps. Consider which is of most value to the organization, which is accessible, and which has the backing of the organization. Then plan to address that need.

- *Sources of expertise* – How do you know how to develop specific needs? There are many ways to find out and to either buy external support or to develop an in-house capability to meet the need, or sometimes, both. What are the advantages or disadvantages of internal versus external support?

- *Sample interventions* – Here are some starters and ideas for ways to develop learning interventions. They range from self-managed through to company-led.

- *Technological interventions* – Two of the growth areas to consider are e-learning and blended learning, which combines multiple methods of delivering learning.

- *Follow-up and bedding-in of new skills and behaviours* – Once employees have learnt, then you need to make sure that they can hold onto the learning and develop it further. How can you be sure that learning is transferred to the workplace and applied?

Roles and responsibilities for learning and development

Learning and development is an organization-wide, strategically important activity. It is the way that an organization ensures that it has the people resources needed to meet its goals and to continue to survive and add value in an often crowded marketplace. Therefore, all members of the organization bear some responsibility for learning and development. Specifically who is responsible for what can become contentious as various people seek to avoid or grab the responsibility for elements of learning and development. I have therefore set out as clearly as possible what I believe the primary divisions of responsibility to be. These will of course vary by organization, but this gives you a template from which to start negotiations.

Leadership

The role of leaders is to:

- *decide* the mission, vision and values of the organization;
- *set* operational plans to meet the mission over a medium- and longer-term period, say 5–10 years on the whole;
- *resource* the learning and development activity in terms of people, budget and time;
- *monitor* the ongoing capability of the organization;
- *review* evaluation of learning and development interventions;
- *interact* with the external environment, spotting changes which require an organizational response;

- *communicate* the need for changes to the HR/L&D function in order to facilitate change.

HR and L&D professionals

The role of the HR and L&D professional in all of this is a central one. It is your role to:

- *Identify* the organizational capability, that is the core process or skill or knowledge that gives the organization its competitive edge, or in the case of third-sector and non-profit making organizations, the capability that allows you to deliver at an optimum capacity. This should hopefully have been identified by the leadership. Frequently it is your role to clarify this capability and record exactly what it is, for example using competencies to define it for the organization with specific behaviours, often in behaviourally anchored rating scales.

- *Identify* the current levels of performance against these capabilities, using operational data, such as achievement against target, market share, attainment levels, etc. Each sector has specific metrics that can be used as a starter to explore levels of capability. This can be complemented with feedback from customers, clients, patient groups, competitors, managers, employees, etc as appropriate.

- *Facilitate* organizational interventions to meet frequent learning needs.

- *Facilitate* the 'people' side of the organization's response to environmental changes requiring a strategic response.

- *Collaborate* with employees to ensure that they understand the development plan and their role in delivering it.

- *Encourage* all stakeholders to engage with learning and development to promote knowledge management and organizational learning culture.

- *Offer support*, advice and guidance to employees in matters of learning and development; for example, brief line managers before their employees attend an intervention, discussing its purpose and potential impact and afterwards supporting them in facilitating the transfer of learning into the workplace. This may involve allowing the individual employee access to specific projects to develop and embed what they have learnt or perhaps giving a learner extra time initially to complete newly learnt skills.

- *Ensure* that they are fully conversant with the specific learning and development requirements of their organization/sector, eg health and safety training issues are frequently specific to a sector. For example, consider the differing health and safety training requirements of a school, hospital and mining facility. The mining facility will have strict rules for health and safety based on physical safety, such as ensuring the atmosphere is safe at depth. Whilst the hospital will focus on hygiene and the school on student wellbeing, they will have very different training needs in terms of health and safety.

- *Evaluate* learning and development interventions on an ongoing basis to ensure that they are fit for purpose, delivered efficiently and effectively and provide a demonstrable and quantifiable benefit for the organization.

Line managers

The role of line managers is:

- *ensuring* that the capability of their team is optimized;

- effectively *implementing* performance measurement and development activities in the team;

- in collaboration with the HR and L&D function, *accessing* appropriate L&D activities to drive individual and business performance;

- *ensuring* fair access and equality of opportunity to all team members;

- *managing* learner expectations, ensuring that they are fully prepared for any learning and development activities and appreciate why they are being given the opportunity to learn and the investment that is being made in them;

- *promoting* transfer of learning on the employees' return or during an intervention as appropriate. This may involve discussions asking the learner to brief the rest of the team and also sometimes to coach those who haven't been able to attend the activity;

- the provision of opportunities to *consolidate* learning;

- *assessing* the outcomes of learning activities and return on investment (ROI).

Employees

The role of the individual employee is to:

- *monitor* their own levels of performance;
- *identify* areas where they need development;
- *actively seek* learning to ensure that they can meet their targets, for example seeking coaching or accessing e-learning;
- *proactively find* ways to develop new knowledge and skills on the job;
- *discuss* opportunities for learning with their manager to ensure they are integrated with the organization;
- *seek feedback* to ensure that their capability meets current and future needs;
- *actively engage* with learning and development opportunities to access all the learning available;
- *actively engage* with performance management systems to identify areas for further learning;
- *give feedback* about learning interventions to both HR and L&D functions as well as to the line manager.

Checklist for roles and responsibilities

Use the checklist on the next page to identify who specifically will meet each of the roles. Whilst they are identified as belonging specifically to one role, you may find in practice that a number of people share responsibility. This first stage in designing and implementing a learning intervention will help you to share the load as well as embedding the intervention in the organization form the very start. This is important, as the amount of support you have will have a big impact on the success of the learning intervention at every stage.

TABLE 6.1   Roles and responsibilities checklist

Role	Primary person	Secondary person(s)
Eg manage learner expectations	J Smith (line manager)	Anon (learning and development practitioner) J P (external trainer)
Set organizational mission, vision and values		
Communicate organizational mission vision and values		
Identify the key competitive advantage and capabilities of the organization		
Identify gaps in organizational capability		
Identify emerging needs for the organization to perform well in the future		
Conduct a learning needs analysis		
Engage with stakeholders		
Plan an ongoing programme to fill the gaps caused by the learning needs		

TABLE 6.1 *continued*

Role	Primary person	Secondary person(s)
Design a programme to meet the learning needs		
Ensure fair access to learning and development activities		
Provide an organizational process for identification of learning needs		
Resource the meeting of learning needs		
Facilitate learning and development events		
Facilitate consistent ongoing learning and development		
Ensure the effective transfer of learning		
Feedback on the effectiveness of interventions		
Evaluate learning and development activities		

Identification of learning needs

This is the core stage of designing and implementing a learning intervention. This stage identifies what actually needs to be learnt. It forms the basis for design of intervention as well as evaluation. This is therefore the key stage to focus on. This stage can be pictured as the identification of a gap in skills, knowledge or ability that needs to be bridged with a training intervention.

When identifying learning needs it is easy to start to focus overly on the minutiae of learning needs that are being identified. For example, in an energy company providing gas to consumers what exactly are the planning skills a service engineer requires? Are they more important than their social skills to engage with customers? What level of planning is required? Or is it more a capability to schedule within a day's work, etc? These detailed questions are very important because the analysis of learning and development needs goes a long way towards designing the intervention, both its content, ie what is taught as well as its delivery, ie how it is taught.

FIGURE 6.1   Bridging the gap between current state and future requirements

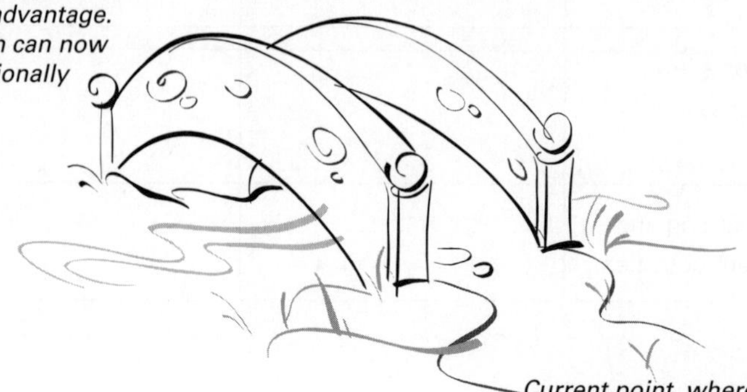

Learning intervention, which is the bridge between current lack of capability to fulfil the organization's mission and future capability. In this example is it a form of blended learning to develop cultural insights and understanding of how business is done in specific international contexts

Destination point, where the organization will be able to fulfil its purpose and maintain its competitive advantage. The organization can now expand internationally

Current point, where there is a lack of skills, knowledge or ability so that the organization is not able to fulfil its purpose. Eg a lack of cultural awareness that prevents it from expanding internationally

Link to organizational strategy

As crucial as this is, it is very important to keep in mind broader issues such as, can these specific skills be learnt or is it essential to recruit for these skills? So, for example, you may consider that social skills are harder to develop within individuals than planning and scheduling skills and so place some form of assessment for social skills as a priority within the assessment procedure. This broader approach to the identification of learning and development needs places them firmly in the organizational and broader environmental perspective. In particular, the organizational strategy should shape the analysis of learning and development needs. This is because the knowledge, skills and abilities of its people are typically the most important resource that the organization has. Therefore their development should focus predominantly on the organizational goals. This information should be taken from formal documents such as policy statements as well as interviews with senior managers. The reason for this is that the strategy of an organization is almost never a unitary, simple focus. Rather, in reality, it tends to adapt over time, with various groups of employees having their own perspective on the strategy, according to their own interests, location and function. Whilst these circle the central strategic intent there is no great difficulty. However, at times they can diverge quite markedly and if you focus your understanding of the organizational strategy purely on a couple of interviews with strategic managers you may be in danger of misunderstanding the core strategy. You could then shape the learning needs analysis incorrectly.

It is good therefore to use a broad range of approaches to understanding all elements of the learning needs analysis. You have a balancing act to perform, addressing the learning needs that you identify whilst focusing on the most important organizational requirements as determined by the organization in the appropriate policy documents as well as senior manager perspectives. If in doubt, for example where the organization is small and does not have a strategic policy, you could look to the mission statement and if that is not yet constructed, speak to the leader of the organization, usually the individual with the title managing director or chief executive officer. You could ask them to project 5 to 10 years ahead to consider the external environment of the business, perhaps using the PESTLE model described in Chapter 5. Then consider how the organization will need to change to meet those needs and finally what knowledge, skills and attitudes will be required to succeed. It has been my experience that senior managers enjoy this process as they are usually forced to react to short-term issues, and so enjoy the chance to think ahead and start to focus on what the organization will need to do.

Organizational perspective

You will carry out the analysis of learning and development needs from within a specific perspective that reflects your place, time and interests. So, you work in one particular section of the organization – this gives you a window into the requirements of the organization, but not necessarily a full picture. You are likely to build better relationships with some people than others; again this gives you a picture into the wider organization, but one that is interpreted through their experiences. The larger the organization the more of an issue this can become. I have experienced getting to know an organization particularly well through good relationships, which meant that I gained a thorough understanding of the organizational learning needs in Birmingham and the north-west of the UK, but less so in London where the senior operational HR manager was keen to maintain a separate identity from corporate HR.

This is exacerbated in an international organization and particularly so when travel is constrained and all conversations happen through Skype or video conferencing. This has the effect of reducing your contact with individual employees. Additionally, it constrains your own perspective on the full range of learning and development needs. It is very important, therefore, to work against this tide in order to ensure full coverage of all parts of the organization, at all levels and with all functional areas. Your own remit may not incorporate an organization-wide perspective. However, you should ensure that one exists, it is up to date and that your work integrates with the broader organizational understanding. The risk of missing out specific areas is in the cost of lacking a full picture. The difficulties this can cause range from alienating one specific employee group who feel neglected, through failure to plan efficiently for implementation, to lacking a business critical skill which may adversely impact the organization at some point.

Systematic approach

One of the primary ways of mitigating this inevitable difficulty is to be systematic in your analysis. Ensure that you cover every aspect of the business in appropriate detail. You could make use of organization charts to ensure full coverage, and meetings with senior managers to ensure that you focus on key areas of interest to them. In a large organization this is an important aspect of gaining support for your work.

There is usually a previous analysis of learning and development needs that you can use as a template. Indeed, your own work may be to update this piece of work. Be certain that you take an evaluative approach to any previous work. Even though you may work with the lead of this previous research, you should take care to think through what was done previously.

Checklist for learning needs analysis:

- Review previous learning needs analysis:
  - Is it still up to date?
  - What changes have there been?
- Has the organization changed focus since the previous analysis?
  - For example, has there been a merger; or perhaps a significant reduction in headcount?
- How effective have previous learning and development interventions been?
  - What went well?
  - What went badly?
  - What was the overall outcome?
  - What is the further learning that needs to be undertaken?
- Review key performance indicators, performance management feedback and any other relevant information:
  - Are there any consistent areas where performance is not meeting target?
- Are there specific areas in which the organization or industry has changed?
  - What sort of performance gaps is this causing currently?
  - What gaps could it cause in the near future?
- What do employees, supervisors and managers think are the key areas for development?
  - Why do they consider these areas to be key?
- Is there a new or emerging part of the business that should be considered as part of a learning needs analysis?

Remember, the primary goal of the analysis is to support the business in its growth and competitiveness. Therefore it is worth being thorough and systematic in uncovering areas for development, even where this may ruffle a couple of feathers.

Most of your analysis work will be based on group information, for example, trawling through previous requests for courses or which competencies were identified as needing better performance in performance reviews. However, it is important to check out your work at various stages by going back to the source to check your initial findings. It is as well to do this during your research simply because time limits will be pressing and checking your understanding as you go along will help to keep you on the right track. You can do this most effectively by meeting up with employees and line managers at various points in the organization. Share your initial findings with them and ask for their feedback:

- Does this reflect their understanding?
- Are there areas that you have missed?
- What do they think will be the main challenges the organization will have to prepare for in the coming few years?
- When they are discussing employee capability with other supervisors what are the main areas for discussion?

This is also an ideal time to begin an initial consideration of how to deliver some form of intervention. You could ask:

- What should be done to meet these learning needs?
- How have they seen it work in the past?
- What are their pinch points, eg in timing – daily, monthly, etc?
- If money were no object what would be the ideal intervention?
- How have they seen these issues addressed elsewhere?

Future facing

Organizations have a history as well as a present and hopefully a prosperous future. Whilst the identification of needs should be focused on the emerging and future needs of the organization it is all too frequently in fact focused on the past requirements. This is because the process involves investigating a range of complex data that typically reports on performance in the past. So, for example, information from the performance management system will be based on what employees have actually done over the past 18 months to two years. This takes into account the time lag before the HR function is able to access the information at a group level, for example anonymizing it and placing it in groups such as cross-organizational service engineers. It is very important to also consider the organization in its environment and look to the challenges it will face rather than only those it has faced. Therefore an analysis of learning and development needs should involve an exercise in considering the next 5 to 10 years of organizational life and the skills knowledge and attitudes that will be needed to excel there. Clearly these should form a progression from those that provided success earlier on. However, there should be adaptations and development to match a rapidly changing external environment. So, for example during the early years of this century it was initially important for an organization to be able to invest well in order to build capability for growing markets and then, suddenly, it became very important for an organization to be able to cut costs and save every form of expense. These two behaviours require different skillsets as well as different mindsets, were business critical and needed to be communicated and developed at pace. Add to this an additional layer that in a cross-border organization some economies will be flourishing whilst others are shrinking.

Sources of expertise

As the facilitator for learning and development interventions, your responsibility is the provision of opportunities to learn. In effect, you are the owner of the process for learning. You should be rigorous in setting up learning opportunities, through assessment of learning needs and also in follow-up through evaluations.

However, the content of what is actually learnt may well be outside your expertise. This should be sourced through others. Your sources of expertise may be external or internal.

External sources of expertise

Professional bodies

Professional bodies are a source of up-to-date expertise. Their mission typically involves advancement of their profession, which incorporates a number of learning resources. They are usually non-profit making. Details for each are available through a Google search.

Examples of professional bodies include:

- Association for Manufacturing Excellence (AME);
- Institute of Directors (IoD);
- Chartered Institute of Personnel and Development (CIPD);
- Chartered Management Institute (CMI);
- Institute of Marine Engineering, Science and Technology (IMarEST);
- American Society for Training and Development (ASTD);
- International Association of Hydrogeologists (IAH).

Consultancies

These are profit-making organizations that seek to provide services through the use of their own expertise. The services will vary according to their area of expertise. These organizations can be costly, but should give access to considerable knowledge and expertise in their area. It is important to source references for them and to ensure that they provide a fair service. You should also ensure that as far as possible intellectual property is shared or owned by you as appropriate and that some of their expertise is transferred in-house.

Universities and academics

Universities may provide education for various groups of employees. For example, executive leadership courses, MBAs and other professional courses which are of high standard and complexity and will provide educations for knowledge workers and leaders. Academics can additionally provide consultancy services and learning opportunities that are highly specialized. They tend to be significantly knowledgeable about a relatively narrow area. Their work tends to be of high status and to also be quite ground-breaking.

Training organizations

There are a number of organizations that provide training services for specific areas, for example health and safety training. Their provision is usually quite standardized and can involve either just one organization or many. The benefits of sending employees on the courses include learning the content of the course as well as picking up ideas from other organizations.

Customers and suppliers

In today's highly networked world, it is not unusual for customers or suppliers to become providers of learning. For example, when a hardware supplier delivers new equipment they will often provide ongoing learning for its correct usage. This is particularly the case with high-tech equipment where the two organizations may in fact design the system together and build a long-term relationship which includes learning on the use of the systems.

Internal sources of expertise

Managers and knowledge workers

These professionals should be knowledgeable about their own areas. They may be able to provide in-house learning opportunities such as induction or products and services training. They may also be able to advise on provision of learning services by other organizations.

Communities of practice

Communities of practice are a very useful tool that could be co-opted by an L&D professional, although they are organic, self-sustaining communities which can act across a number of organizations as well as within organizations. They are essentially a loose affiliation of individuals with a common interest who collaborate over a fairly long period of time. They share learning, insights and challenges and may also build solutions and innovate together.

However, communities of practice are also rigorous and focus on a specific domain of interest. You are likely to be a member of a few communities of practice. For example, if you are an active member of your local branch of the CIPD, perhaps you are a talent management specialist, involved in a cross-functional specialist group, such as focusing on recruitment strategies in your organization.

A community of practice is also very much a community – it involves regular interaction, whether face-to-face or online, socializing, support and shared activities. The essence of the community of practice is that members are practitioners, seriously involved in their chosen area, who develop their practice through social interaction.

The L&D function can support and facilitate this very valuable form of learning, for example by setting up websites or wikis that members can use, facilitating the use of organizational facilities. This can prove particularly useful as it enables organization members to be active parts of the community of practice. As they develop their own practice, so the organization benefits. Additionally, by creating a link between the organization and the community of practice, the organization can become linked to good practice and the desire for learning built on the part of employees as they see that good practice is valued by the organization in both word and deed.

These communities are not static and cannot be constructed – only encouraged. Their membership is likely to evolve over time and individual members may move between being central or peripheral members depending on their current circumstances.

Internal versus external provision for learning and development

As a learning and development practitioner you face a choice between providing learning and development internally that is tasking an employee with designing and delivering the intervention or engaging an external provider. Each of these is appropriate to specific situations and each also has pros and cons. These are laid out in Table 6.2.

There is another approach to the provision of learning which is to allow the external and internal provisions to complement each other; for example, engaging with an external provider and including the development of internal staff as part of the contract. This allows for employee development, design of a bespoke service, retention of intellectual property and can ensure that the organization's specific culture and approach is attended to for more effective transfer of learning. When combined with multiple methods, this is also known as blended learning.

Blended learning

Blended learning is the provision of a curriculum of learning through various modes of delivery, for example, face-to-face group briefings, individual study using e-learning, coaching, group-working or using social networking forums. This allows a more individualized approach that also allows experts to facilitate discussion of more complex questions. Perhaps using self-study through e-learning to cover foundational learning with challenges through facilitated small group sessions and practical work to develop skills, with learning demonstrated by using skills whilst being observed by a coach. Blended learning is also highly focused on the learner, who has the freedom to decide how to blend methods, such as choosing to engage with forums on social media rather than reading a book.

TABLE 6.2 Comparison of the costs and benefits of internal and external provision of learning and development

Internal provision of learning and development	External provision of learning and development
Advantages:	Advantages:
In-depth understanding of the organization, culture, mission and way of doing things	Expertise and capability for specific learning area
In-depth understanding of products, services, customers, etc	Breadth of experience and understanding across industry
Typically lower cost	Expert status, greater acceptability and willingness to learn
Available once set up	A fresh pair of eyes can pick up on issues that employees are blind to
Transfer of learning is more effective, partly as facilitator is on hand to support	Flexible in adapting sessions to time and slots available
Bespoke to the organization and designed solely for its use	Where individual employees attend events, there can be significant learning from other delegates
Development of capability among employees who facilitate the learning	External provision is more likely to led to recognized qualifications
Potential to cascade learning throughout the organization	
Disadvantages:	Disadvantages:
Can take time to develop capability	Capability remains external to the organization
May lack expertise	May become dependent on provider
Solely a one-organization perspective may be parochial	Typically higher cost
Status of the employee facilitating the intervention will limit its potential for more senior employees	Lead time to book further sessions, follow-up, etc
Initial set-up costs may be high due to need to develop both capability and design course	

The benefits of blended learning are:

- It is cost-effective.
- It provides an individualized, learner-centric approach that allows learners to work at their own pace.
- It provides flexibility, which ensures that learners can develop whilst continuing to perform their roles in the organization.
- Learning can be undertaken without significantly undermining the work-life balance.
- It meets the different learning styles of individual learners.
- It meets the requirements of a diverse range of learners.
- It can support multi-location learning, enabling integration of learning across global workplaces.

The difficulties of blended learning include:

- Learners need to be self-directed.
- Evaluation is complicated by the multiple methods used.
- There may be an overdependence on e-learning and learners need to be proficient in the use of technology.
- It can be complex to implement, with an increased requirement for tracking learners' attendance and progress.
- The organizational culture of learning and development may need to adapt to meet this new approach, eg allowing learning whilst sitting at the desk and not seeing it as an added perk or shirking.
- Facilitators can have increased demands as learners call on them as and when they wish.

Models of blended learning

Models of blended learning are primarily designed for educational settings, such as colleges. These may have a value for the workplace, but are not always the most appropriate. The difficulty with blended learning is in the breadth of the concept, which encompasses almost any form of learning. Models attempt to define more clearly specific types of blended learning:

- *Lab rotation* – where learners move in and out of a lab and classroom. What is taught in the classroom is informed by what is experienced in the lab so that classroom sessions become more of a seminar. This is most appropriate for skills learning, for example, use of an accounting package that must be administered accurately and efficiently or perhaps in a call centre environment.

- *Self-blend* – this is where learners are particularly motivated and active in their learning and direct their own learning. This is usually initially from a suite of resources provided by the organization, which the learner uses as a starting point for further exploration of their area of learning.

- Graham (2012) has identified models of blended learning that operate at specific levels within the organization, including activity, course, programme, institution:

  - *Activity level blending*: this involves using multiple types of activity to support learning within a single intervention.

  - *Course level blending*: this involves the use of different 'modules' of learning, using various methods that together, used over a range of times, places and media incorporate the learning intervention.

  - *Programme level blending*: this involves the use of multiple methods for a whole course of learning. For example, in the development of a graduate population, working towards a professional exam, multiple learning methods may be used.

  - *Institution level blending*: This is where institutions work together to deliver learning. Examples include executive development programmes where the participants are from multiple organizations, the educational element is delivered by a business school and the experiential elements are delivered by some of the participant organizations. It may involve a formal collaboration between organizations, for example a group of hospitals and a university may collaborate for medical training (Bonk and Graham, 2012).

Sample interventions in learning and development

Short-term learning

Induction

This is the process of onboarding new employees. It aims to get an employee integrated within the organization and working effectively in as short a time as possible and lasts between a couple of days through to a couple of months for particularly senior roles. It is also part of building the employer brand and starts to engage the new employee with the organization. Each organization has their own process that reflects their culture and sector. Typical 'ingredients' include:

- introduction to induction as part of a welcome pack prior to joining the organization;
- timetable for various meetings during the first couple of days;
- HR meeting for pay and benefits;
- products and services training;
- health and safety briefing.

Product training

This skills and knowledge-based process focuses on specific products that an employee will interact with as part of their daily role. The focus of this intervention is to upskill the employee in as efficient a manner as possible. Therefore, selection of employees to attend this training is important. It often involves exercises to prepare for the training as well as follow-up exercises to embed learning afterwards. The training is usually face-to-face, depending on the products. For example, electrical engineers may have to demonstrate competence with a new piece of equipment and be signed off as having competently performed a task before being allowed to use that product.

Briefing on HR processes

A core part of the annual cycle of performance management is briefing on HR processes. This is usually delivered to local teams by the line manager. It includes an outline of the process, how employees should prepare for their own appraisal and often a discussion of the development opportunities following an appraisal. It usually also involves a discussion around the pay and benefit changes that may follow an appraisal, for example, performance-related pay increases.

On-the-job training

This is perhaps one of the most common forms of learning and development and involves a more experienced employee demonstrating specific tasks to a newer employee. It has the benefit of being fine-tuned to the learner's requirements, delivered just-in-time and at minimal cost.

Job rotation or secondment

This form of development is frequently used early in a learner's career, or when they are seeking a change in direction. It may be carried out between collaborating organizations, for example supplier and customer or complementary suppliers to one customer, for example in the car industry. It typically involves either a few days a week or a period of perhaps a couple of weeks through to six months. Employees swap roles in order to gain a better understanding of the other person's perspective and to understand their role better. It is an approach that I experienced as a young graduate. I spent a few days in each department of my organization. It gave me a much better understanding of how the organization as a whole worked as well as an appreciation for roles in other departments.

Longer-term development

These are learning and development activities that take place over an extended period. They frequently involve an educational element and in some cases, such as mentoring, may build supportive relationships that last for years. There are a wide range of long term learning and development activities, some of which are described here.

Self-managed learning

Self-managed learning is a process of learning devised by Ian Cunningham (1999) who describes it as 'almost like group mentoring. Such groups need to consist of five or six managers who create their own learning agenda. The group usually requires a skilled learning group adviser to make it work'. Bennett *et al* (2000) note that it is 'about individuals managing their own learning. This includes people taking responsibility for decisions about what they learn, how they learn, when they learn, where they learn and most fundamentally why they learn'. It involves an adaptation of action learning which is suitable for a broad range of employees. It engages with the motivation of employees to develop themselves and gives them the tools of time and mutual support as well as in some cases budget to achieve their learning goals.

Self-managed learning operates in sets and the role of L&D is to act as facilitators for the set. Initially, it is useful for the L&D specialist to be part of a set in order to fully understand how it works. The sets consist of usually between 8 and 12 employees from various parts of the organization. It is important that they are a diverse group who do not work together on a day-to-day basis. A learning set should not be comprised of one function or department, as the existing relationships between people are likely to dominate the conversation and prevent genuine learning. The set should meet for a limited time, say two hours every month for a year. This limited time focuses the concentration of those in the set on the learning.

The process of a self-managed learning set is:

1 *Agree a contract for the learning set.* The contract is a way of managing the set. It includes the ground rules of how the set will work. For example, when and where will the set meet? How frequently? What are the confidentiality rules? How will the learning budget be divided up, etc? The facilitator should take a leading role here in ensuring that everyone is comfortable with the learning contract. It should also be explicit that each learner is accountable to the set for his or her learning and the set will challenge their learning if they feel it is not rigorous enough, or too rigorous.

2 *Start a learning audit.* Having been chosen to form a set, the next step is to meet and start an audit to identify learning goals. This should include the individual learner's preferences for what they learn, their manager's preferences, any professional or standard requirements and discussions with others, perhaps through a 360-degree questionnaire, performance review, etc.

3 *Identify learning goals.* Set members agree learning goals based on the audit. These should be SMART, ie specific, measurable, achievable, realistic, time bound. Each one's goals are discussed among the set. The set should challenge goals where they think there is some more work to be done. Also, at this stage each member agrees the initial steps to accomplish their learning.

4 *Work towards learning goals.* This is the main part of the set experience. The first three steps should take up a couple of meetings. Now, the bulk of the learning starts. The sets form a repetitive pattern of each meeting, every member presents back on their learning over that period. They are likely to discuss the challenges they encountered, what they did about them and where they are now. The set should respond in a supportive and yet challenging manner so that the 'perfectionist' is challenged to accept sufficient learning and the 'slacker' is challenged to try harder. There may be input from specialist speakers where members share learning goals. In this phase the facilitator

should be carefully monitoring how things are going, encouraging and supporting the group as appropriate and ensuring that everyone has a fair share of airtime. It is not unusual to find that in some meetings one of the members takes up more time as they have a specific need. This is fine, as long as the facilitator manages it.

5 *Confirm learning through achievement.* The learning that has been achieved over the period is recognized by the set. There may be portfolios of work, or projects achieved. The explicit outcomes of the learning will vary a great deal by what people have learnt and how. For example, someone taking up a position supporting Latin America may have learnt business Spanish and their confirmation of learning could be a seminar given in Spanish, with a translation. This confirmation should include a summary for each individual of the learning that they have achieved. For some groups it is useful to have a senior manager present to acknowledge their learning on behalf of the organization.

6 *Close the set.* The final set meeting is a celebration of what has been achieved which allows a process of dispersal of the members. Ritualizing this process, for example by sharing a meal, enables the members to move on more easily. Close relationships are likely to have been forged and whilst they will remain, their nature may change as the setting for meeting will also change. This is also where the facilitator bows out from close involvement in the development of each group member to allow them space to work with another group.

Crucially, the group must be facilitated by a facilitator who will observe, clarify questions and support the group. Cunningham (1999) notes a number of issues concerning the qualities and role of the set advisor, which centre around the need for them to be impartial, independent and skilled. The role of the facilitator is to:

- select members of the set;
- set up the initial meeting;
- keep the group on track;
- maintain rules of confidentiality;
- ensure that all members are equally included;
- source support for the group, eg in the form of budget or occasionally specialist speakers;
- facilitate the closing of the set after it has run its course.

The benefits of self-managed learning are in its cost-effectiveness and also in the quality of learning achieved. As individual learners are self-motivated, they will use every opportunity to learn, which ordinarily may need to be attractively presented or packaged. For example, they will be likely to conduct their own 360-feedback review, conduct their own reading and bring that learning back to the rest of the group. The evaluation of the group ensures that the learning is to a high level and will engender further learning. This learning, to the specific requirements of the individual, moderated by their manager, will therefore transfer more easily to the workplace and quickly build capability there. A further benefit is in the quality of cross-organizational relationships that can enable various pieces of work to be facilitated in the long run as employees from diverse parts of the organization know one another well and can support one another in finding a way to get things done.

Where successful, a self-managed learning programme can be very popular among employees and L&D may well need to bring in selection criteria for joining a set. These criteria should focus more on the learning requirements and less on previous educational attainment or seniority in the organization. Otherwise, a set can become a badge of honour. The first set I belonged to was a trial of the process and membership was a badge of honour as it was facilitated by the L&D director. This created a difficult atmosphere in which people did not want to reveal their real difficulties to their line manager and had a very limiting effect on the learning achieved.

Coaching and mentoring

These are both more informal interventions in that they are usually organized to suit the employee in terms of scheduling and often the content of discussions.

Coaching

Coaching involves a one-to-one relationship that focuses on issues that the individual coachee presents. The coach may be internal or external and the coaching may be quite long-term or for a specific number of sessions. The coaching may also be carried out by a line manager. More recent developments have incorporated the use of coaching for teams to help build team focus and improve working relationships.

There are two main types of coaching:

1 *Developmental* in which an in-company coach, often the line manager, supports the employee in the development of competencies

of solving specific issues. For example, where an employee has difficulties with behaviours such as assertiveness or persuasiveness then a line manager coach may spend some time working through the issues with them and perhaps also sourcing resources to help.

2 *Executive* in which a coach (usually external to the organization) supports a senior manager in enhancing their performance. He or she acts as an independent listening ear and can provide feedback to the manager, challenge their perceptions and provide support for working through particularly difficult issues.

A useful structure for a coaching session is the GROW model developed by Graham Alexander in the 1980s:

G – Goals. What does the individual want to achieve?

R – Reality. What is actually happening now? What is the backdrop?

O – Options. What options are available to the individual?

W – Way forward. What is the individual willing to commit to and what is an agreed way forward?

This structure can be used for a 10-minute corridor conversation where necessary, if someone catches you unawares and you do not have the opportunity to set up a proper session. It is also useful for a longer coaching session with all the correct safeguards such as confidentiality agreement.

Mentoring

Mentoring typically involves a relationship, usually but not always set up through the HR function. The more senior employee shares their knowledge and understanding of the organization, function and sector to support the more junior mentee in their development. This can include a broad range of issues including discussion of issues around how to manage their direct line manager, how to be a line manager, socializing into more senior levels of the organization and knowledge, for example industry knowledge. From a learning and development perspective it is particularly efficient as it is learner-centric and supports a reflective and experiential learning perspective. The mentor can act as a sounding board for the mentee, enabling them to think through difficulties and make good choices.

The mentoring relationship tends to be quite long-term and they can last for years, building up genuine, mutually supportive relationships. This is one of the reasons why care needs to be taken in the selection of mentor and mentee. It is also important to start the relationship with training/briefing sessions on its purpose and boundaries as well as some consideration of coaching-type skills.

Benefits of mentoring include:

- The sharing of tacit knowledge across organizational boundaries.
- It can give more senior managers a realistic sense of what is actually happening on the ground.
- It can build working relationships both across levels and across functions where both parties are in different functions.
- The costs of mentoring include initial training and use of resources, primarily people and premises – less than other interventions.
- For a high flyer it can build up long-term mutually beneficial relationships.
- It is adapted to the specific needs of the mentee and so is a more efficient source of learning.
- It develops people skills in the mentor, eg listening, encouragement, challenge, etc.
- At an organizational level it is a strong plank in both a learning organization and also provides for good knowledge management.

However, mentoring does not always run smoothly, primarily as it is based on a working relationship between two people. Issues may arise around the availability of the mentor, particularly if they are someone very senior and it may not be in the organization's interest to take up the time of particularly senior people with too much mentoring. The choice of mentor and then the selection of mentee to work with them is very important. It can also happen that the mentee is 'starstruck' and unable to build a good working relationship, as they are intimidated by the mentor, simply because of their seniority. This is an issue of particular concern with mentoring as it is based on a trusting, honest and proactive relationship on the part of both parties.

Continuing professional development (CPD)

Continuing professional development is a typical requirement of any professional and so needs to be actively considered by the learning and development function. It involves an ongoing consistent maintenance and development of the individual's practice, to ensure that their work is fit for purpose.

CPD is typically measured through the counting up of hours or points with an annual target decided by the relevant professional body. It is typically planned through the development of a learning plan or personal development plan. A sample personal development plan is included below. This very simple layout demonstrates the essentials and should be adapted and personalized for your own use.

It is the responsibility of the individual to ensure that they access sufficient learning to achieve their CPD points. However, it is useful for the learning and development professionals to facilitate this learning as it enables them to ensure that it happens, direct it towards areas of particular value for the organization and build it into relevant performance management mechanisms.

TABLE 6.3   An outline personal development plan

Learning goal	Activity	Success criteria	Date	Comments
To improve capacity to influence across levels of management	Stakeholder analysis of the core clients	I will persuade senior managers x and y to change their approach to an employee issue	XX/XX/XX	I spent time with my manager reviewing this. She added some comments and indicated how I could use it further
To improve capacity to influence across levels of management	Application of stakeholder analysis to new management assessment programme	I will persuade senior managers x and y to change their approach to an employee issue	XX/XX/XX	It is very useful thinking about how to approach senior managers. I will focus initially on the marketing manager as she is very open to new ideas and has been through something like this in the past

There are a broad number of ways in which CPD points can be collected:

- reading around the subject;
- attending webinars and seminars;
- undertaking a formal course of learning;
- attending professional service companies presentations, eg presentations on employment law given by law firms looking to raise their profile;
- attending the meetings of professional bodies such as the CIPD;
- e-learning;
- mentoring by a more senior professional;
- targeted coaching to deal with specific issues;
- membership of a LinkedIn specialist group;
- challenging projects in the workplace;
- secondment to another function/organization for a short period;
- attending a conference;
- joining a self-managed learning group.

Reflective practitioner

Once an individual has completed some of their CPD activities there is one further highly valuable activity that should ALWAYS be undertaken. That is reflection. Taking the time to mull over what went well, what went badly and what you would do differently next time is a way of making the most of the learning. It allows the learner to suck dry every single piece of learning. It also enables them to learn from mistakes and avoid them in the future. Initially, reflection needs to be guided; a useful model to structure your thinking initially is double loop learning, which encourages a reflection on achievements and difficulties as well as underlying assumptions.

Donald Schön (1983) devised a practical and insightful model of reflective practice. His seminal book *The Reflective Practitioner: How professionals think in action* is a very useful guide to reflective practice. It also outlines some of the philosophies that Senge (2006) picked up on in devising the concept of the learning organization. His model is both profound and simple and formed the basis also for Agyris's (1974) work on double loop learning described earlier.

The essence of Schön's model is reflection in two different arenas:

- *reflection in action;*
- *reflection on action.*

Reflection in action

In the heat of the moment, when conducting a performance interview, meeting with managers or trying to solve a tricky problem it is easy to become embedded in the situation and somehow forget ourselves. Schön encourages individuals to think on their feet and reflect on the situation as it is happening, eg has this happened before? What are my expectations here? What does the other person really want? How am I responding to this? What could I try out to improve the situation? We are then in the best possible situation to respond to the events unfolding as they occur.

Reflection on action

Once the events have passed, then an individual should take some time to think about what happened. This should be done within a relatively short space of time, perhaps on the journey home that night or on the journey in the next day. It may involve a discussion of what happened with team members, manager or mentor and perhaps a review in the CPD record. In particular it is useful to think through exactly what happened, your response in the situation and afterwards, responses others may have had, where that leaves the project and what should be done next.

This stage is unique to the specific individual and situation. It may be that on a change in role that the individual spends a great deal of time in structured reflection, which later will be unnecessary. It is also specifically useful for a team to use when planning activities and options that it may use in developing its capabilities.

You may find it helpful to look back at Agyris's (1974) double loop learning on page 94 and consider how you could build reflective practice into your daily activities.

Technological advances in learning interventions

E-learning is a way of delivering learning that brings with it many opportunities. E-learning is a catch-all name for any learning that is delivered electronically. It is a fast-moving arena that allows organizations to individualize learning to a much greater extent. Learning interventions may be synchronous in which all participants are engaged at the same time. Examples of this include a webinar, which is a web-based seminar in which an expert shares their knowledge with a group. E-learning may also be asynchronous in which participants engage in the learning in their own time. An example of this is the learning provided by the Open University. This happens at a range of levels and across all areas. Participants undertake modules, which they complete at their own pace, with tutor support, within a broad timescale. Qualifications can be earned using this approach.

Examples of e-learning include:

- *Web-based training* – The learning is delivered to the learner who is likely to be alone and does not interact significantly with any others. Typical examples of this include induction training. This enables the organization to ensure that the new employee has taken in the learning through the use of end of unit tests that are recorded by the HR function. This is particularly useful where health and safety issues are involved.

- *Supported online training* – The learner interacts with the tutor and others supported by online content as appropriate. Typical examples of this include skills training, such as use of logistics software or webinars in which one instructor is meeting virtually with a group – all of whom are logged in but in different locations.

- *Informal e-learning* – Here the learner uses technology to communicate with others and learn during normal hours. This is a particularly powerful form of learning as it is focused on the workplace, partially led by the learner who is able to adapt it to their needs. This makes the likelihood of its being used far higher and additionally means that it absolutely meets their specific needs. Much of memory is context-dependent and by learning during normal hours in the usual workplace the learner is more likely to recall the learning and therefore further enhance its stickability. Tools to be used include wikis, blogs, etc.

- *Use of social media* – Social media is a very diverse and fast-growing arena that impacts all areas of HR, learning and development included. For example, in 2013 the use of LinkedIn as a means to identify potential talent is very strong. Social media is differentiated form other forms of e-learning, as it is users who generate the content. Therefore, it tends to suffer less from the difficulty of appearing static, old and irrelevant, which a very expensive 'learning zone' on the company intranet can easily fall into. The use of social media can be uncomfortable for an organization because of issues around control. For example, it can seem that any analysis of learning needs becomes irrelevant as employees access their felt learning needs through the suggestions and ideas of peers. There may also be issues of control around intellectual property and confidentiality of organizational business. These need to be carefully considered and managed through HR policies and processes. For example, it may be possible for an organization to make effective use of SharePoint or Yammer, an organizationally-based Facebook. This allows social media whilst keeping it in-house, enabling cross-organizational work which is particularly effective for project-based work.

- *Collaborative learning* – This is learning in which the participants work together on a specific problem given to them by an instructor. Examples of its use include online case studies that enable participants to manage elements of a business so they can see the implications of their decisions within a controlled time frame. It is also useful for skills development as participants together seek the optimum solution. This type of inductive learning, which is led by participants, tends to enhance their learning and deepen their understanding.

  Collaborative learning may also be used as a form of organizational learning where social networks such as Twitter are used to share ideas. These focus particularly on the use of 'social capital' that has been built up through a trusted network so that people are comfortable sharing ideas. These ideas are then able to be worked on collaboratively, to bring benefits at a whole range of levels. For example, looking at how to develop a graduate population, a Wikipedia page could be set up by a graduate to allow discussion of how things are, what development they would welcome, organizational feedback, etc. This sharing of learning incorporates reflection as well as building up a shared body of knowledge 'from the ground'.

Benefits of e-learning

There are many benefits of e-learning including:

- It is available as required and can be used continuously for learning and reference.
- It is flexible for access to be made available anywhere and anytime.

- The training can be delivered consistently for a consistent learning experience. In the case of qualifications this is an important consideration.

- It is efficient and can reduce the time it takes to deliver learning.

- It is very recordable so learning activities can easily be logged by the organization as well as the individual employee for continuing professional development (CPD).

- The interventions can be individualized for each learner through varying delivery patterns to create a bespoke learning experience.

It is very useful for MNCs to encourage organizational learning that includes employees who work in disparate locations and normally would not interact because of the distance between their locations and their jobs not usually requiring contact. This helps support the development of a coherent organizational culture and cross-organizational relationships. For example, graduate trainees from different parts of the globe may be required to work on an e-project together, developing business awareness, cross-cultural awareness skills and organizational knowledge.

It is inclusive in its delivery as it can be used by all employees regardless of any mobility difficulties or other disabilities as well as employees who are part-time or work on shifts.

Difficulties with e-learning

However, there are additionally a number of difficulties with e-learning:

- Depending on the provision used, there may be start-up costs, which for small organizations could be disproportionate, leading them to reject the e-learning option.

- Line managers need to be engaged with both the content and delivery and encouraged to support its use.

- There is a need to distinguish carefully between formats appropriate for hard learning, for example of knowledge, and soft learning, for example about interpersonal skills.

- The current technology infrastructure is limited and although growing rapidly still limits what is possible.

- When learners attend a training course then the organization can be sure that they are present and attentive. However, on-the-job e-learning is very easy to put off and allow other tasks to overtake it. By allowing the learner to lead, the organization has lost some of the control of the learning. It can be moderated by giving the learners a timescale in which to finish the learning. However, it is still up to the learners to ensure that they have been diligent in completing the learning. For essential learning it is therefore advisable for learners to attend away from their usual workplace, or to ensure that they are supported by their line manager.

- The need to provide support is a barrier for e-learning. Whether that is through line managers or the provision of time, the learner may be exposed to hostility from the rest of their team who have to do extra work while they learn.

- The learners themselves may be hostile to the e-learning. Attending a course has many benefits that are attractive to employees, including time away from the usual workplace, good food, a break from home and the opportunity to mix with new people from across the organization. E-learning removes all these 'perks' as well as adding additional pressure in the form of hostility from work colleagues.

- The organization may miss benefits of cross-organizational relationship-building. This can ease the functioning of the workplace and whilst not usually acknowledged, may also be sorely missed when it is not in place. It is a form of implicit knowledge-building that can make an organization function more efficiently.

- It can be difficult for organizations to source attractive, relevant and high-quality content. This is important as the other web-based interactions that the employee undertakes, including leisure activities on the internet, TV, etc are very high quality.

- The employee may lack the IT skills to access the learning effectively.

E-learning may be most effective when used as part of a blended learning approach. This uses a range of every available mode of delivering learning, for example, a course in a training centre, some e-based learning, discussion groups, private reading, etc. The options are almost endless and allow for an individualized experience that ensures learning is optimized and transferred to the workplace.

E-learning is a fast-moving area. Some high-tech organizations use elements such as wikis to encourage learning on the job at the same time as product development. It could be delivered through iPad, Kindle, gaming formats, social media-based smartphone technology, apps, cloud-based technology, etc. The options appear currently to be limitless and it is through pilot studies and experience that organizations will be able to find the best format for their specific requirements.

One area for caution is the difference between the potential that a new technology may have and the rate of take-up among employees. It is important for organizations to continually monitor usage rates to determine the value of technology-based learning. This may allow ongoing adaptations, for example such as when and where employees can access the technology to ensure take up. Otherwise, it may be in danger of becoming a very expensive white elephant. For example, it is noticeable that on commuter trains a majority of commuters while away the journey watching a downloaded TV programme. This appears to be an excellent opportunity for them to watch some form of training video such as a TED excerpt. However, it may be that at this time of day they just want to switch off from work and whilst being offered the opportunity to enhance their knowledge, may reject this opportunity in the interests of work–life balance.

Follow-up and bedding-in of new skills and behaviours

This is one of the core areas for learning and development. Learning is a process that cannot always be fitted onto a timetable. Therefore, opportunities to extend the learning through preparatory work and follow-up are useful. Blended learning is particularly useful in this area as it allows the learner to proceed at his or her own pace.

Some areas are more difficult to learn than others. Changing behaviour is particularly difficult and often requires consistent follow-up over an extended period. Structured feedback is particularly useful for embedding learning as it enables the learner to identify glitches and work on them during the daily work. This hugely increases the chances for the learning to stick and simply become their usual way of doing things.

Feedback

Feedback is one of the primary tools for learning and development. It allows the learner to measure their own performance and has a number of applications:

- It increases self-awareness, for example for a learner to begin to understand that there is a problem. A supervisor may have an unduly brusque approach that he is not aware of. Feedback may enable him to appreciate the impact of his behaviour.

- It supports transfer and maintenance of new skills and learning. Once the initial burst of energy on the part of both individual and organization has passed, degradation of skills and knowledge can happen rapidly. Perhaps a colleague demonstrates a short-cut which renders some of the learning irrelevant, or an individual may mis-remember part of one session.

- It helps learners gauge where they should focus their primary efforts in developing themselves.

- It enables the organization to get a better picture of how people are really doing, for example, through the performance management system.

Feedback should be specific and closely related to the task that the learner is engaged on. For example, when considering complex technical machinery, such as gas installations, giving specific feedback related to the quality, accuracy and speed of installation. The learner should have clarity on the gap between desired performance and their current levels of performance. The feedback should be specific, clear, positively termed and usually include remedies to help the learner bring performance levels up to standard.

FIGURE 6.2 Illustrating 360-degree feedback

360-degree feedback

As its name suggests, 360-degree feedback is effectively a process of the learner holding up a series of mirrors to view his or her performance from angles that he or she usually doesn't see. This involves asking for feedback from a 360-degree circle, ie everyone that the individual interacts with. The format of this varies; some prefer a more structured survey approach which gives some degree of confidentiality to the respondents as responses are usually averaged and summary responses are given to the individual. The difficulty with this is that the individual learner can be left wondering what the significance is of, say, four out of seven on a scale about flexibility. Without specific examples and further detail the meat of the feedback has been lost and the exercise is less than useless. This is compounded by a central tendency that respondents often have when they do not want to be overly generous or harsh and so stick to the centre of the scale. However, a more open-ended approach can end up simply being a review of the learner's reputations and personal characteristics.

Once an exercise like this has been carried out ineffectively, an organization usually becomes hardened to the activity and quite resistant to future attempts to bring in a similar approach. However, where there is a strong development culture then it may be possible to ask for rich feedback, with specific examples of the issues that are raised. With sensitive feedback this can prove an extremely valuable source of personal awareness, the precursor to personal development. In particular, themes can be drawn from the feedback to identify where issues arise, for example because of procrastination. The individual learner then has clear targets for development once they have digested the feedback.

Making the case

For those of us engaged with learning and development, who see the difference it makes in people's lives, there is no need of persuasion. However, organizations must make difficult choices so it is important to provide a rational, clear case for managers to be able to make effective choices. This is useful as it also helps you in making the best choices for learning activities.

You should initially gather support through discussing the potential learning needs with a broad range of stakeholders and seeking their ideas for the 'shape' of a learning intervention. They may have specific requirements of time and budget, which it is helpful to know early on.

When you are ready, it is important to make a professional case, perhaps providing a written business report and accompanying presentation. You should access your previous work on identifying the learning need in order to demonstrate:

- the specific learning need;
- how it relates to the business goals;
- why the activity is required;
- costs that may be incurred by the intervention, including budget, people, time, etc;
- how the business will benefit;
- exactly who in the business will benefit from the development;
- onward benefits, eg improved processes, enhanced employee engagement.

It is also useful to carry out a pilot study to be able to weed out any glitches. An early demonstration of success is more likely to persuade budget holders to use their resources for this activity.

You should also develop a communications plan to ensure that those interested are able to ask their managers to attend and to communicate the successes of the activity. This will build your own reputation and that of the function, which will ease setting up future activities.

TABLE 6.4 Comparison of methods of learning and development

Method	Learning need	Seniority of learner	Type of organization	Comments
Blended learning	All types	All levels	Appropriate for all types of organization	May need to be facilitated carefully
Face to face	Skills and complex knowledge	All levels, less usual for top managers	All types	This type of learning is less transferable so care should be taken

TABLE 6.4 *continued*

Method	Learning need	Seniority of learner	Type of organization	Comments
Coaching	On the job and attitude/skill	All levels	All types	Coaching is a very skilled activity; for more senior roles and where a skilled coach is not available, external coaches should be used
Mentoring	Organizational knowledge and understanding	Primarily professionals and managers	Medium-sized up	Mentoring needs to be carefully facilitated
360-degree feedback	Behaviours	Junior manager upwards	Medium-sized up	Needs to be carefully facilitated as feedback can be destructive if not handled well
Self-managed learning	Knowledge, skills and behaviour	Those keen to develop	Any size	Requires careful facilitation and management support

CASE STUDY

Verona Diagnostics is a producer of diagnostic tests in the area of fertility. They have a strong reputation in the industry for reliability and provision of good support services for their customers. The consequences of any errors in their production and diagnostic processes are high, for example false negatives where patients are informed that they are infertile or not pregnant when in fact they are and also false positives when patients are informed they are pregnant or fertile when they are not. This includes some complex fertility issues that require high levels of skill and expertise to assess. Verona Diagnostics has a zero tolerance of error.

Eighteen months ago they relocated to consolidate their provision just outside Verona, Italy. The move was as smooth as could be expected with employees having 18 months' notice, fair selection of employees offered relocation and generous redundancy terms with outplacement support for those made redundant.

However, whilst 100 per cent accuracy of both instrument and analysis is a known standard, since the move to Verona, accuracy rates have dropped to between 89 per cent and 100 per cent. There have been a number of discussions surrounding this difficulty, which is having a negative impact on the organization's brand image and needs to be resolved as a matter of urgency. The graph below indicates the accuracy levels attained since the move to Verona:

FIGURE 6.3 Chart of accuracy rates for production and inspection

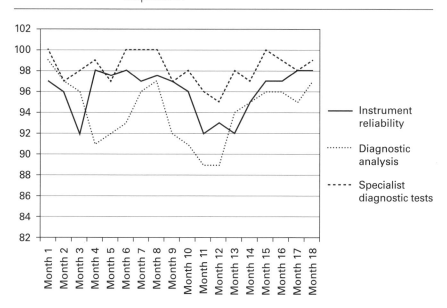

These results are unusually poor for Verona Diagnostics and significant management time has been invested in trying to understand why they are so poor.

Learning needs analysis

A learning needs analysis was conducted to understand the causes of the gap. The learning need analysis was an in-depth analysis of:

- initial job analysis;
- performance review data;

- customer complaints;
- records of errors by:
  - type, product range, details of the issues under investigation;
  - frequency, how often, day and time of day;
  - circumstance, team membership, product and which shift pattern.

Results

Its primary findings were:

- The move to Verona for employees was highly distracting and as a result of the change in environment the maintenance of complex skills was not as effective as prior to the move.
  Environmental issues were having a negative impact on employee accuracy, in particular poor lighting in the redesigned laboratories and fatigue due to lack of natural light and change in shift pattern.

- Disruption of team relationships meant that employees were less comfortable asking team members to check their findings, resulting in higher error rates.

Recommendations

There were a number of recommendations that flowed from the analysis. Verona put time and resources in place to close the gap between desired levels of performance (100 per cent accuracy) and actual levels (89 per cent up). There was a focus on developing an open culture of ongoing learning and honing of skills. Interventions included:

- Refresher training sessions to prevent skill degradation. These included short simulations of novel and less-usual slides for inspection, bi-weekly for two hours. These were conducted in an open learning environment of discussion rather than a testing environment, and requests for further support and questioning of decisions on slides were encouraged.

- The role of team leaders was enhanced to include further on-the-job learning, with coaching for team members on an ongoing basis.

- Team meetings were established on a weekly basis for ongoing refresher training, for example, by discussing errors during the previous week and how to ensure they were prevented in the future. These are to be used as an opportunity to develop a learning approach to errors in order to encourage a culture which values learning and sees mistakes as an opportunity to learn. Team meetings should also include a motivational element in which the implications of errors are occasionally discussed, with case study examples.

- Trialling different shift patterns and upgrading the labs and the lighting in particular.

Conclusions

The initial outcomes of this study and its recommendations were accuracy rates of between 97 per cent and 100 per cent. This is a significant improvement that Verona discussed in detail with its primary clients who had started to become dissatisfied with the service. They were encouraged to comment on the expurgated findings of the needs analysis and discuss how to ensure skill maintenance and development. This helped to build closer relationships with clients. This was an added benefit of the learning needs analysis, which had not been initially expected.

Gantt chart to plan development of a learning intervention

Table 6.5 on page 182 shows an outline Gantt chart showing the major steps in the design of a learning intervention. These steps are the essential core and will differ in various situations. It aims to give you an idea of the major steps involved at a practical level in developing a learning intervention. Some activities focus on building organizational support, some on evaluation and some on designing activities. The timescales are also very approximate.

DIAGNOSTIC QUESTIONNAIRE   To identify
strategic areas for people development with senior managers

Introduction

This questionnaire is an outline for you to adapt for your own purposes.
The structure of it should be used as a whole, but could perhaps form the
structure of focus groups as well as interviews. However, depending on
your sector and organization, the individual follow-up questions may be less
relevant. When preparing for the interview, think through the sorts of factors
that impact your sector and adapt the questions accordingly. For example, in
the pharmaceutical industry the American Food and Drug Administration is
a body with defining importance; other industries will have less need to pay
heed to international legislative bodies.

Structure

1   Welcome the manager and explain the purpose of the discussion.

2   Thinking about our organization and the external environment in which
    it operates, how do you think the international economy will change in
    the next 5 to 10 years? In political terms, what do you see happening?
    How will that affect our industry? How will that affect us, eg if the
    administration changes will there be different lobbying rules?

    –   In economic terms, what do you see happening? How will that affect
        our industry? How will that affect us, eg how could we respond to
        a sudden growth in overseas demand?

    –   In social terms, what do you see happening? How will that affect our
        industry? How will that affect us, eg what are the social trends that
        might impact us, such as the drive for better ethics and corporate
        social responsibility?

    –   In technological terms, what do you see happening? How will that
        affect our industry? How will that affect us, eg how will technology
        change the way we communicate with our customers? How could
        we use technology to engage customers?

    –   In legislative terms, what do you see happening?
        How will that affect our industry? How will that affect us,
        eg are there new trends of legislation that could impact us,
        such as trade union laws, health and safety laws, etc?

- In environmental terms, what do you see happening? How will that affect our industry? How will that affect us, eg is there a change in climate around us? How could it develop over the next 10 years? What could we do to respond?

3 Finally, if these are the ways that the broader external environment will change – what do we need to do to develop ourselves and our people in order to meet the challenges? What do we need to do next? What are the priorities?

4 Thank you very much for your help. Is there anything I have not asked that you think is important? Would it be possible for me to contact you later if I have any other questions?

DIAGNOSTIC QUESTIONNAIRE
To develop learning interventions

1 What is the overall purpose of the intervention?

2 What are the specific learning outcomes required?

3 Who is the learning aimed at? What are their characteristics, eg age, gender, disability, specific issues expected, prior learning, expected degree of motivation to learn?

4 What are the stakeholder expectations, eg champion, management, learners, employees, providers, others?

5 What is the time frame? Budget? What other resources are available?

6 What are the sources of resistance and support for the activity within the organization?

7 Who do you have to support you in the development of the activity?

8 Which methods are you interested in using/are available?

9 Should learning be in a group, with an instructor or alone?

10 How will the learning be best delivered, eg convergent – focusing on learning specific facts such as learning the rules of lifting heavy objects or divergent, exploring the links between facts to build a rich picture such as using a case study to explore ethics?

11 How will you pilot this activity?

12 What is your communication plan for this activity?

TABLE 6.5 Gantt chart of possible steps in a learning intervention

Activity/date (week)	1	2	3	4	5	6	7	8	9	:	:	:	:	:	:	:	:	:	:	:
Learning needs analysis	▓	▓																		
Confirm specific learning needs with stakeholders			▓	▓																
Identify resources and activities				▓	▓	▓														
Engage experts/support to design learning							▓	▓												
Pilot learning									▓											
Review pilot and adapt										▓										
Roll out learning											▓	▓	▓	▓						
Evaluate learning									▓	▓	▓	▓	▓	▓	▓	▓	▓	▓		
Communicate successes																		▓	▓	▓
Design follow-up											▓	▓								

Measurement

07

Introduction

Learning and development experts know that it is important to evaluate and usually have good intentions to do so. However, in the hurly-burly of managing the function, they may either let it slip, or choose a complex range of metrics, which becomes untenable. Evaluation is important as it demonstrates the value of the learning and development activities. It should be carried out against organizational performance indicators and stakeholder requirements.

Measurement of learning and development activities aims to provide an evaluation of their effectiveness. Specific questions that evaluation can answer include:

- Which elements of our programme did not really work – no matter how good they felt?
- Which were effective during the activity, but didn't really have an impact in the workplace?
- Which were the surprising success stories?
- Which have worked in only one region/country/part of the business? And why was it received so differently in different parts of the world?
- How much better is performance after the training?
- How long does the improvement last?

Evaluation is divided into two key parts:

1 *Measurement of the intervention and its effectiveness in enabling learners to access learning, knowledge, skills, attitudes, behaviours.* This form of measurement is very difficult as it must always be imprecise – except in some specific areas of technical training, the

learning will be internal and to measure it we must rely on indirect reports. For example, how do you measure the effectiveness of coaching? Do managers provide the best insight, or direct reports? Or perhaps the learner themselves – but can they really have full insight into all of their behaviours? There are a number of conflating factors such as how the amount of work, or tight deadlines, or difficulties at home impact the quality of coaching. These are so many and varied that to measure the specific skills of coaching is very difficult.

2 *Evaluating the value of the learning to the organization.*
The most effective, elegant and well-resourced intervention may be of little real value to the organization if it delivers learning no longer required. The inverse is also true so an informal, 'back of an envelope' intervention may be just what is needed. Of course, organizations are less likely to evaluate the back of an envelope intervention so they may never know how well it works!

This chapter addresses some of the fundamentals of measuring and evaluating learning and development, identifying practical tools to help practitioners in evaluating their own organization's application of learning and development. It also aims to understand how to evaluate learning and development when you are delivering interventions internationally. It will discuss why evaluation of learning and development is so important, and so often neglected. It will then review a range of approaches to evaluation. These vary in their applicability according to the type of organization you are in as well as the type of learning.

Why evaluate learning and development?

In leading an agenda for learning and development it is very easy to be busy at providing a range of interventions to ensure that primary learning and development needs are at least met. There is a security and also a sense of satisfaction in being able to meet with senior managers with a well-designed presentation detailing who has done what in following up their development needs. However, this is no guarantee of success in changing people's levels of skill, knowledge or attitude. The focus of your activity should be the far more nebulous and less easily defined actual increase in skills, knowledge or enhanced attitudes and improved levels of behaviour.

Evaluation has additional benefits of demonstrating the value that learning and development provides. It demonstrates utility and added value. Certainly this provides some protection during a recessionary part of the economic cycle when learning and development are first on the hit list for cost reduction. It is also highly motivational. Often in learning and development we 'plant seeds'. Evaluation demonstrates which of those seeds have blossomed and benefited others, which can be a huge boost for the team, providing an opportunity to celebrate work, as well as demonstrating the value of the work to others.

The use of evaluation is applied to varying degrees in different organizations and locations. Huque and Vyas (2008) note acerbically: 'evaluations by clients of training services in the public sector do not receive serious attention as one cohort of officials succeeds another'. By contrast, in the charity sector evaluation is recognized as a central part of demonstrating the effective use of each donated amount. Additionally, the United States tends to be less focused on evaluation of learning and development than parts of Asia.

There are a range of models and approaches to evaluation. Each is appropriate to a specific situation and can be used to both assess how effective the learning has been and to demonstrate the value of the learning to more senior stakeholders. The process of evaluation aims to put the learning and development in its full organizational context, considering the onward benefits of the learning. This has the impact of enabling the organization to compare the value of various learning interventions and so identify the most valuable and use resources for optimum benefit. This can be used to improve ongoing learning interventions and also to choose between various programmes, supporting the most effective and ending those least effective.

However, the process of evaluations is fraught with difficulties at a number of levels. For example, the obvious requirement will be to demonstrate that the intervention caused an improvement in some form of skill, knowledge, attitude or behaviour. However, it is really only possible to show a relationship, or a correlation between the intervention and the outcome, not that the intervention itself caused the improvement. The reason for this is that the conditions required to enable causation to be established are usually experimental. For example, in medical studies, some participants are given the actual drug on trial, whilst some are given a placebo, usually a sugar pill. No one knows who is taking which drug so that the outcomes, in terms of who gets better and who does not, can be more clearly linked to the effects of the drug itself. It is a very forgiving organization that would agree to pay for an intervention, 50 per cent of which they knew was ineffective, or a placebo. Therefore, this form of experimental research is very rare indeed and we must satisfy ourselves with alternative forms of evaluations that indicate a relationship rather than demonstrating a definite effect.

How to evaluate learning and development

One decision that needs to be considered is at what point will the learning and development be evaluated? Perhaps you would prefer to check learning prior to the intervention itself. Ideally, this should have been done as part of the needs analysis. You will therefore have specific expectations about the level of capability you are expecting in your participants. The effectiveness of this form of evaluation varies according to the subject of the learning. For example, if the purpose of the training is to develop IT skills, say in Excel and Word, then the current level of capability is very easy to measure using a short test. This could be repeated, with a parallel test (which measures the same capability but using different questions) at the end of the intervention, say at the end of the training session. This would give a very clear measure of what the participants had learnt and how their levels of skill had changed. You could repeat a parallel test at some point in the future (say six months) to see how much they remember and perhaps add a short questionnaire to understand how it has changed their use of IT in the workplace. This gives a clear measure of both the effectiveness of the intervention as well as its utility, ie did it work and was it worth it?

The simplicity and value of this approach depends very much on the subject matter. Where a work-based, universally applicable skill such as use of IT is involved, evaluation is less complex. However, evaluation of, for example, a management skill such as coaching or delegation is far more complex. Here, the checking of learning prior to the intervention is in many ways a formative evaluation. That is, it enables both the participant as well as the provider of learning to understand the current levels of skill. For a complex and quite abstract area such as coaching this is invaluable. You may start, for example, with a videotape of the participant coaching an errant employee as a starting activity. However comfortable they perceive themselves to be, once they have watched the tape back, they are likely to understand far better their own behaviour and motives and so be more receptive to the learning itself.

However, coaching is a skill that can be learnt as a structure in an intervention, but takes a long time to become a proficient part of a manager's toolkit. It is very much related to individual differences and the manager's own style of working with the team. It is therefore far less accessible to evaluation. At which point should the intervention be measured – immediately afterwards; after a month; five years? Perhaps a manager will not even have totally finessed the skill of managing through coaching on retirement! How can the coaching be measured in the workplace? Perhaps through 360-degree feedback – but this is an indirect measure which is fraught with the motivations and perceptions of the various respondents. Coaching itself is also very context-based and as a highly skilled activity varies both from person to person and also with the nature of the coachee. Therefore the evaluations must necessarily be 'in the meanwhile' – that is imperfect but still useful. However, as measurement is so imprecise, so the utility will be under-reported. The relationship between a somewhat undefinable vague measure and an indeterminate end point will be muted because the lack of precision of the measure leads to a broader range of scores.

Where a programme for intervention is lengthy, for example, aimed at all middle managers across a large organization, then it is reasonable to evaluate it whilst it is in process. This form of evaluation enables improvements to the programme as it runs. These may be less central to the content of the intervention, for example, changing venue or timings. However, it may also involve a change of learning material or styles in response to ongoing feedback. It is important that each participant receives the best learning experience possible. However, an unintended outcome of this is that evaluation becomes much more difficult and the goalposts keep changing. However, it is perhaps even more important to evaluate each iteration to ensure that the learning experience remains powerful, even where it is less comfortable. As the champion of the learning event you may find yourself having to defend it where participants have not enjoyed certain elements that are essential to the learning. This is usually the case in managerial learning events where feedback to weaker managers can be quite painful at times. It is important to hold on to the original vision for the training and allow the managers to work their way through the pain in order to learn fully.

Models of evaluation

Benchmarking

Benchmarking is a technique used across industry to identify good practice and measure organizational performance against it. Benchmarks are essentially the goals that organizations set themselves that are usually derived from competitor performance. They are particularly applicable to learning and development as they can be assigned for specific interventions, types of intervention and learner groups. For example, it may be possible when using external trainers for a skills course to benchmark your group of learners against others in your industry, eg considering speed of skill development for retail customer service assistants compared with those in other retailers. This use of group data enables you to consider how your own learners and techniques compare with those of your competitors. This is a rich source of information that helps to highlight the effectiveness of learning and development, even where your own provision is only for a few learners. The primary difficulty of using benchmarking is in sourcing information about other organizations. Typically, it is necessary to use a third party, either an industry forum of some type, perhaps through a professional body or a tool designed for benchmarking.

An example of one tool designed for benchmarking is the WLP Scorecard, (which can be viewed at **www.wlpscorecard.astd.org**). This is an online tool for benchmarking at a number of levels, including industry, type and size of organization and type of intervention. A thorough tool, it promises confidentiality and which is recommended by the American Society for Training and Development (ASTD). They identify the main purposes of the tool as:

- to monitor and benchmark a broad range of learning function, financial, operations, customer and innovation indicators;

- to customize reports with subsets of organizations and indicators;

- to compare the alignment, efficiency, effectiveness, and sustainability of an enterprise learning function, as well as the overall quality of the learning function, with other organizations;

- to diagnose strengths and weaknesses in variables that affect alignment, efficiency, effectiveness, and sustainability;

- to perform sensitivity analysis to see potential effects of adjustments to multiple variables on alignment, efficiency, effectiveness, and sustainability;

- to make decisions about all aspects of learning, including investments, staffing, processes, and the type and amount of formal and work-based learning opportunities

Kirkpatrick's levels of evaluation

The most frequently cited model of evaluation is Kirkpatrick and Kirkpatrick's (2009) model, which identifies four separate levels of intervention:

1 *Reaction* – How do learners feel about what they have learnt immediately after delivery?

2 *Learning* – How have their skills, knowledge, behaviour/attitude changed?

3 *Behaviour* – How has the learning changed the way they do their jobs?

4 *Results* – What is the impact on the functioning of their part of the organization?

This model is often criticized for being out of date and certainly it is simplistic. However, it is this simplicity and its focus on practical application that makes it an appropriate tool for practitioners as the technicalities of evaluation can be very complex. This can be a deterrent for practitioners and if the task is too technical and complex there is a danger that evaluation will not be carried out at all. Certainly, in the past I have noticed that evaluation can be more noticeable by its absence. Kirkpatrick's levels therefore have a great advantage in their simplicity in that they are usable.

The purpose of evaluation is to work out whether the changes that are seen in the workplace are caused by the learning and development interventions and ideally to separate out the elements that were particularly effective as well as those that were not. This can then be fed into the next delivery of this particular course. This can be very complex as well as time consuming. Additionally, the levels are not causally linked; success at one point, perhaps the immediate reaction of those who have just enjoyed a two-day course, does not imply anything about the effectiveness of their learning.

1 *Reaction* – which deals with the immediate response to the intervention from the participants. Usually measured with 'happy sheets' it simply considers how the participant feels at the end of the intervention. More than anything it is a form of customer satisfaction measure and can become somewhat overinflated in its importance.

Although, at the same time, it is the learning achieved that is particularly important and if a learner does not enjoy the experience they are far less likely to engage with the learning itself. There is nothing worse than being stuck in a training room, listening to a boring trainer drone on when there are a million things to get done in the workplace. The chances of actually learning when the learner is unengaged are really quite low.

For those delivering the intervention, measuring delegate reaction can almost become a measure of popularity and likeability. It can also be overemphasized as it gives numbers and percentages that are subtly deceptive because they give us something to report! However, the reporting is of how participants felt – not how effective the learning was. Whilst a pleasurable experience will be likely to make participants more open to the learning, it is merely a step in enabling learning and says less about the learning itself. Although, the negative effects of a poorly received intervention, especially on recruiting future participants, should not be underestimated.

2 *Learning* – focuses on the gaining of skills and knowledge. It is usually expressed as a test of some form at the end of the intervention or shortly afterwards. Used in an educational setting, for example towards professional exams, it is a form of summative assessment that tests what participants have learnt. It is very important for some types of learning. For example, apprentice gas fitters must be checked to be sure that they know the safety details of their job in enough detail before being allowed to visit customers. However, it is less useful for interventions focusing on complex interpersonal skills such as coaching, which we discussed earlier, on page 162.

This level of learning is closely linked to the content of the intervention, ideally designed through a rigorous identification of learning needs. This therefore is a key point for evaluation as it assesses whether the learners have achieved the learning objectives that were the point of the intervention. It is useful to spend some time considering when to assess this level of learning. A majority of interventions occur in stages – for your intervention, would it be better to assess learning at each stage, or to combine some stages? The benefit of evaluation at this point is that you can be fairly sure that it is the learning that has made the difference. This is not always the case with other levels of evaluation.

3 *Behaviour* – considers transfer of learning to impact behaviour and performance in the workplace itself. This evaluation essentially starts to consider the value to the organization – once learners are back in the workplace – how much of what they have taken on board will be transferred to be used in the workplace? There are a broad range of factors that can impact the transfer of behaviour, for example, does the learner have a chance to practice their learning? This is essential for skills learning in particular – if a learner does not have the chance to practice their skills, for example a trainee nurse learning a medical procedure, then their learning is likely to degrade rapidly.

The tricky part is to work out when to measure this – the longer you leave it the more other factors may conflate with your training. For example, an employee may have received considerable coaching and support from a more experienced employee so you cannot be sure how much of their capability is due to the intervention and how much is due to additional support afterwards. However, measure this too soon and the employee may not have had enough time to practice and finesse their new learning, so the evaluation may underestimate the effectiveness of the learning.

4 *Results* – consider the ongoing impact of the intervention. What has been the measurable impact on the organization? How can you demonstrate an improvement? Is it in improved customer satisfaction or reduction in faults? Often, results are very difficult to measure, for example there may be significant benefits from improved teamworking once everyone is working at the same level of capability following the learning.

If the intervention has been designed with the capacity for evaluation planned in from the beginning, then there should be a way of identifying improvement in even the most intangible of areas. For example, there may have been an initial opinion survey of employee or customer satisfaction prior to the intervention. This could now be repeated to measure any differences. Other areas of results that could be considered include the number of customer complaints and the cost to the organization of making good any errors, grievances and absenteeism, levels of employee engagement, levels of turnover and so on. These will be specific to the workplace and a great deal of time and consideration should be put into choosing the metric and way of measuring the results.

Context, input, reaction, output (CIRO) (*Warr*, et al 1970)

Context, input, reaction, output (CIRO) is a framework for evaluation that allows for a systematic process of evaluation of programmes as well as distinct learning and development interventions. It incorporates both operational and strategic perspectives to consider why you would want to carry out a specific learning intervention and how to do it for the best outcome. The information they provide is discrete and allows for comparison across different locations for delivery. Therefore learning can be evaluated at a range of different applications and compared. This allows fine-tuning of corporate interventions, for example to local cultural needs so that a learning and development intervention can be effective both globally and locally.

For example, an international retailer may have a system of supply, which they brief all employees on, and train the local buying team. However, for a western team, the focus may be on achieving good prices, whilst for a more collective culture, the focus may be on building trust. By using CIRO these differences in acceptability of the pace of negotiations can be identified and the interventions adapted to allow for both local cultural requirements and an organization-wide system.

This approach to evaluation is useful to demonstrate how learning and development achieves specific business objectives and so enables you to build a business case for the work. It takes a more holistic approach to consider the intervention from a number of different perspectives, starting at the beginning of identifying the need through to its longer-lasting impact.

Context

- Have needs been identified correctly?
- Have accurate objectives been set?
- Does the intervention match the organizational culture? Does it feel comfortable for people?

Inputs

- How well has it been planned?
- Have resources been used efficiently?
- Is the intervention cost-effective?
- Have the learners been selected properly?

- Have the learners been briefed correctly on the development they are to take part in?

Reactions

- What are the reactions of learners? Did they enjoy the sessions?
- Was their learning facilitated by the atmosphere of the location? For example was there enough space? Was lunch on time/tasty/sufficient, etc?

Outcomes

At an appropriate time following the intervention (which will vary a great deal depending on the type of intervention and learning) consider:

- What are learners doing differently now?
- Is that enough of a change?
- Is the change sufficiently established?
- What could be done differently to gain a greater learning?
- What methods can you use to assess a change?

Relevance, alignment, measurement (RAM) approach to evaluation

The RAM approach focuses the analysis of learning and development on the outcomes that the organization may experience. It is based on research carried out by the University of Portsmouth and the CIPD. It considers three specific areas to analyse:

1 Relevance;

2 Alignment;

3 Measurement.

Relevance

This addresses business issues and concerns. It focuses the specific challenge that the learning is designed to address on specific business requirements. This approach aims to ensure that the business can effectively be built up to meet its competitive challenges. It asks questions such as:

- What are our current skills and talent gaps?
- What are the competitive challenges we are aiming to meet?
- What emerging challenges are we considering?

- Where is the business most effective and how can we build on these strengths?
- Where is the business least effective and how can we develop talent in these areas?

Alignment

This addresses the practical issues such as budget and time constraints to build a practical intervention that can be measured against organization realities.

- What do stakeholders specifically require of this intervention?
- Who else do you need to communicate with?
- What are the budget and time constraints?
- What are the specific business metrics that need to be measured?
- How can this intervention be benchmarked against other organizational learning interventions?

Measurement

This ensures that evaluation is not an afterthought but is embedded into every element of the intervention, from initial design through the learning itself and onto longer-term business impact:

- How can we demonstrate the value of the intervention qualitatively – how it has helped build business capability?
- How can we demonstrate the value of the intervention through numbers, such as reduced turnover, improved customer satisfaction, improved sales, shareholder value, meeting client requirements, etc?
- Are there specific metrics that could be used to demonstrate the value of the learning, such as KPIs (key performance indicators) or ROI (Return on Investment)?

Collaborative evaluation

Frequently, learning and development practitioners are focused on building resources for their own organizations without consideration of what is happening across other organizations. This is an area in which it may be useful to begin to consider collaboration both within your own sector and also across industry. The chances are that you are not the only organization using the specific intervention that you wish to evaluate. By joining forces with other organizations you may be in the position to carry out a more rigorous evaluation that will help to uncover the true underlying benefit and difficulties of the intervention. For example, you may be using a form of customer service training. The outcomes of this may be affected by issues such as the quality of training, timing or locations of training, the previous learning or participants, etc. In other organizations these factors will be different. By combining your data you will effectively cancel out the impact of individual factors such as location for training and identify the underlying factors leading to a successful intervention. For example, does follow-up training help to transfer the knowledge so that customer service assistants are more effective and customer feedback is typically more positive?

Clearly, when liaising with other organizations there are sensitivities, particularly if you happen to be liaising with competitors. However, the benefits to be gained from this sort of collaboration in enhancing the learning and development outcomes are considerable. Given the difficulties commonly associated with evaluation, this type of collaboration should be seriously explored.

CASE STUDY

Amrat is the learning and evaluation manager for a third sector organization, Fight Multiple Sclerosis Now! (FMSN!), which provides education around identifying the early signs of multiple sclerosis (MS) as well as raising funds for MS research. The organization employs 150 people: 20 per cent in the head office, 15 per cent in publicity and 65 per cent in direct educational interventions. The majority of learning and development involves work-based skills as well as management training. The organization also sends employees on specialized leadership and also sector-specific skills courses. It is highly accountable as all their funds come in the form of donations. It is therefore essential for them to demonstrate prudent use of funds whilst operating as efficiently and effectively as possible. They additionally have specific constraints concerning their status as a charity. They are used to providing an evaluation of all their services, particularly for the use of major funders such as trusts and private estates. Therefore, evaluation has become part of the culture of the charity.

Amrat's role incorporates evaluation of all the activities of FMSN!, as well as learning and development. He uses evaluation for all L&D interventions and focuses usually on the CIRO approach. He describes this as sufficiently flexible to use across most types of learning. He also relies on provider-led evaluation for externally based provision, but tends to review the evaluations rigorously and has been known to question claims very closely.

Amrat also works to benchmark learning and development activities with other charities. As members of the sector they share similar issues and concerns and freely share information and other resources, as far as intellectual property issues allow. Amrat has started an invitation on Wikipedia to compare learning and development interventions across the organizations populated by third sector organizations. This has proved popular and more people have asked to join. There are now 130 contributing members, each from different organizations and each specializing in learning and development. Bob has remained in tight control of the Wikipedia page, ensuring that the members are genuine and asking for an evaluation of one element of their learning and development offering as an initial posting to the Wikipedia. He believes the core benefits of the Wikipedia page are a sharing of honest opinions about providers, sharing of best practice and innovations and also sharing difficulties. Amrat was a recipient of some helpful advice when a recent delayering exercise put two members of his team at risk. Through his evaluation work he was able to demonstrate the value of their contribution and gained useful suggestions from members of the Wikipedia page.

Individual evaluation

We have discussed evaluation primarily from the perspective of the organization. This is because as they receive the invoice it seems that they should be the ones to check out the value of the learning intervention in achieving their strategic goals. However, the individual learner is also a recipient of the value of the learning and should therefore take part in some form of evaluation for themselves. In fact, it is an essential part of extending and embedding the learning to ask the individual to review it. It can also be a very useful part of embedding learning. The typical areas that learners may be asked to evaluate include:

- *Before the intervention:*
  - How am I doing currently on...?
  - What are the areas of... that are a particular strength for me?

- What are the areas of... that are an area of development for me?
- What do I particularly need to change for my current role?
- What would I like to be able to do in...?

- *During the intervention:*
  - How did I respond to that session?
  - What was the key learning?
  - What has confused me/seems muddy?
  - What would I like to learn more about?
  - What do I need to practise more?
  - What did I already know/access without difficulty?

- *Immediately after the intervention:*
  - What did I enjoy?
  - Why?
  - What did I not like?
  - Why?
  - What are the main things I will work on now?
  - What are the specific goals for implementing this learning in the workplace?
  - Who will notice the difference?
  - Who can support me in the workplace?
  - Who could I ask for feedback about how I am improving?

- *At intervals after the intervention eg two weeks, two months, six months as appropriate:*
  - How well am I using what I learnt?
  - How has it changed my performance in the workplace?
  - What else would I like to learn about this?
  - If I am not 100 per cent happy with my performance in this area – what else can I do to develop?
  - Is my ongoing learning to do with behaviour, skills, attitude or knowledge?
  - What self-directed learning can I use to support this, eg reading, feedback, coaching, etc?
  - How has my development been evaluated in the workplace?

As with a group evaluation, such as an organization-wide evaluation, so individuals may consider their levels of effectiveness prior to, during and after the intervention. It can be especially useful to consider the value of the intervention over longer time frames. For example, using the subject matter of coaching that we discussed on page 162, a manager may find their feet with coaching in one team, but struggle on changing another team. They may also intermittently wish to review their coaching style to understand whether in adapting it to their own style they have lost some of the effectiveness. This ongoing evaluation is in itself a form of continuous personal development as the reflection itself will aid self-awareness and so direct the focus of development.

These individual evaluations may, under certain circumstances, also be collected as group information in order to contribute to a group-level evaluation. Following the circular nature of this area, they may also be useful as input to the next learning needs analysis. This is particularly the case as they will typically provide a more sophisticated level of self-understanding and so a higher level of learning needs, which have incorporated initial learning and are now looking at next steps.

Evaluation of leadership and management development

Evaluation of interventions at leadership and management development is as important as with all other learning and development activities. Essentially, it highlights the degree of effectiveness of the interventions, the extent to which it is aligned with the strategic goals of the organization and the efficiency with which it is performed, ie is it cost-effective, does it provide value, taking into account the resources it uses?

However, the difficulties of evaluation are extended in this area of learning as:

- the population undertaking this form of learning is usually much smaller, the data available for evaluation are therefore more open to being skewed by individual circumstances;
- the interventions are usually more individualized, reducing further the capacity for comparisons;

- the seniority of the learners makes evaluating their learning problematic and political factors frequently come into play which make evaluation enormously sensitive;

- the purpose of the learning is often more holistic and directed towards individual capability as a manager rather than specific skills. Therefore more indirect forms of measurement may be appropriate, such as the success of that manager's function. However, a greater number of conflating factors come into play, which make evaluation even more difficult to undertake.

Evaluation of leadership and management development therefore should be undertaken from a broad range of perspectives to accommodate the difficulties identified above. These can include:

- the individual learner should be encouraged to reflect on their own learning:
  - where they were before the learning;
  - where they are now;
  - the extent to which the intervention supported their learning;
  - the extent to which they were able to access the learning;
  - what they need to learn next.
- 360-degree feedback, particularly if conducted before and after the intervention;
- the views of the facilitator, HR professional, learning and development professional;
- KPI/business results for their area;
- assessments undertaken by the learner and change following those assessments;
- awarding bodies, eg ACCA, CMI, CIPD.

Evaluation of coaching

Evaluation of coaching is particularly tricky as both input and output of coaching are imprecise, variable according to the situation and very difficult to define. Even where coaching is highly focused on a specific issue and delivered over a tight timescale, difficulties remain. For example, the issues raised are usually very specific and the path for development is also highly individual. However, difficulty in evaluation does not imply a lack of value. It is important therefore to use more qualitative techniques such as interviews, 360-degree feedback and the like to estimate the value of this type of intervention.

Evaluation at an industry level

Some of the difficulties of evaluation can be accommodated using academic techniques for evaluation across industry. These approaches allow a rigorous evaluation of a range of learning and development interventions. The increase in number of participants means that the effectiveness of the interventions can be measured quite finely. These evaluations can be accessed through academic journals or industry magazines such as the *Training Journal* or *Personnel Management*. They should also be evaluated at a local level to ensure that they apply fully. However, if you are considering starting a new intervention, such as interviewing skills or perhaps a form of management development, then a trawl through the literature to see what has worked for people in the past is usually a good way to start. The CIPD website and also the *Training Journal* are good places to begin.

Evaluation through big data

Evaluation has, until very recently, involved a focus on measuring what an organization chose to measure, for example, setting up a survey to measure response to a specific learning intervention and then repeating a similar survey six months later to see how much of the learning has been retained. However, through social networking – Twitter, Facebook and so on – there is now a huge amount of data that can potentially be mined for HR purposes. For example, an in-house social networking site could be reviewed for comments concerning courses. Additionally, HRIS (human resource information systems) can be designed to capture significant amounts of data that demonstrate the ongoing effectiveness of learning. In larger organizations they could capture information on the variations in effectiveness of an intervention on a national basis. This will be particularly useful for an organization that is building a common culture in an international setting, for example setting a common managerial culture whilst ensuring that managerial skills are concordant with local laws and norms.

There are significant ethical issues to consider here, including data protection, confidentiality, etc. However, this area is in its infancy and there are likely to be significant gains for the whole area of measuring human capital, including evaluation of learning and development.

International variations in evaluation practices

In 2010 the CIPD carried out a survey of learning and talent development practices in Asia, covering mainland China, Taiwan and Hong Kong. One of their key findings was that evaluation of learning and development is a more consistent practice in Asia and is also carried out more thoroughly. They note (CIPD, 2010) that while globally only 1–5 per cent of learning and development interventions are evaluated, in the Asia Region:

- more than one-third measure the actual outcomes against expected outcomes;
- over 50 per cent actively link key performance indicators with learning and development;
- approximately 20 per cent carry out return on investment and cost-benefit analysis;
- one quarter investigate the qualitative aspect of the impact that learning and development has had on individuals;
- roughly 60 per cent assess the expectations of managers on the return on learning and development interventions;
- around 44 per cent assess managers' estimation that individuals would benefit from the learning and development activities.

Utility of learning and development interventions

Utility looks at the value that learning and development offers the organization. For example, will the development need still be there after the intervention? How did the development need arise? For example, it may be that induction will always be essential for new starters to introduce them to the company culture and the way things happen in the organization. However, there are some forms of development that shouldn't necessarily be repetitive, for example, salespeople's understanding of contract conditions.

Quantitative measures of evaluation

Quantitative measures of evaluation are both highly attractive and also deceptive. They provide a number to play back to the organization that demonstrates the benefits the L&D has brought to it. They appear objective and unassailable and can provide a measure that though appearing 'solid', can also be over-interpreted. In effect, the number is only as good as the parameters you have chosen to measure. There are three particularly useful measures that provide the mirage of objectivity:

1 return on investment (ROI);

2 payback;

3 cost-benefit analysis.

Return on investment (ROI)

Return on investment provides a measure of the gains earned through learning and development. It directly compares the costs, measured financially, with the benefits, measured financially.

ROI = costs/benefits.

Costs may include:

- time developing the intervention;
- time attending the intervention;
- cost of the facilitator;
- administration costs;
- venue costs;
- material costs;
- costs of managerial support and coaching to transfer the learning;
- opportunity cost – of what else the function and the learners could have been doing during this time.

Benefits may include:

- improved organizational processes/knowledge;
- increased customer satisfaction;
- reduced error rate;
- improved product quality;
- improved levels of employee satisfaction;
- increased employee retention;
- enhanced management skill;
- increased revenue/profitability.

Skills evaluation

The evaluation of skills is an essential part of both skill development and skill retention. Skills can degrade over time and in particular for those roles where skills are essential, such as pilots; then a regular check that skills have been maintained is essential. This may also be seen as a development intervention in itself. Skills are also a useful place to compare different methods of learning and instruction to see which are most effective for a particular skill. For example, when training gas fitters, is a classroom environment most useful, or should job-based coaching in the form of an apprenticeship be the preferred method?

Knowledge evaluation

The evaluation of knowledge becomes increasingly important in today's economy due to the speed of development. For example, knowledge of the best use of computer systems can be outdated within six months. Therefore, for knowledge-based organizations ongoing evaluation through performance management and then a benchmarked approach to compare knowledge with competitor organizations is likely to be particularly useful.

Behaviour and attitude evaluation

The evaluation of learning and development interventions for areas around behaviour and attitude is particularly problematic. This is because our definition of the behaviour and attitudes is extremely complex. In addition, behaviours and attitudes presented in the workplace are also highly complex. Consider the apparently simple task of setting a departmental budget – a manager has completed this before and so it seems like repetition. However, the manager must engage with changes over the previous period in order to set a fair and robust budget. This may be challenging as the manager will be choosing where to spend resources as so must be alert to the specific needs of those in their department. Therefore the simple task of setting a budget becomes a complex identification of merit against need, a 'guestimate' of future business trends and a political choice as to where to place resources.

This is where self-managed learning can be particularly effective. The measurement of the effectiveness of the interventions is carried out by the group itself as an ongoing, iterative process. Whilst the degree to which this can be shared across the organization is limited by the confidentiality agreement, it can be accessed indirectly through asking the group about the relative effectiveness of the different interventions that they used.

Bennett *et al* (2000) note that, 'people are self-managing anyway... people can be sent on courses, and to that extent controlled, but they will choose what they learn... managers may go on a course about being better learners... but within a few weeks they are behaving in exactly the same way they did before attending the course'.

These forms of evaluation are also the start of the intervention as they act as a learning needs analysis. The process of development and learning is somewhat circular, with the end goal being ongoing improvements in individual, team and organization performance.

CASE STUDY

Ed. is a telecom provider across Europe and the northern states of the United States. An internationally known name, Ed. provides telephony services to both consumers and businesses. In their business division they have a persistent development area that concerns salespeople overselling. It appears that in the heat of the moment, and with the desire to make the sale and build their own conditions, they are willing to agree to terms for the client which can sometimes make the deal unprofitable for the organization or promise technology that is not yet available or call data records on ridiculously short timescales that the business billing systems cannot provide.

The HR business partner for this area, Dawn, carried out some research to understand why it was happening. She carried out critical-incident interviews with some of the salespeople and also benchmarked their issues with other providers, through her HR contacts. She also spoke with the in-house lawyers who had frequently complained of trying to unpick promises made by sales, which could put the organization into a loss-making position on its deals, as the penalties for failure to meet the promises are typically very onerous and squeeze already-tight margins.

Working in collaboration with the management team, in-house legal department and an external facilitator, Dawn set up a short series of seminars. These had two objectives:

1 teach the salespeople the core issues concerning contract law and the key deal parameters to which the business could sign up;

2 facilitate an upskilling in negotiations so that the salespeople were better armed to negotiate effectively.

This was followed up with half-day sessions and materials to guide sales negotiations further designed by the salespeople themselves in collaboration with the in-house lawyer. This development was additional to the extensive training put in place for new salespeople. The question therefore arose of how worthwhile it was.

Dawn carried out an evaluation which made use of the 'RAM' approach as well as uncovering the utility and ROI of the investment in development.

Relevance

The current skill gap was clearly in terms of negotiation skills. However, Dawn also considered the need to develop senior management skills in the head of the sales team as well as adapt the bonus scheme to include a profitability component as well as a bonus for direct sales. The benchmarking ensured that the business was competing effectively in this area and, in Dawn's opinion, they were stretching ahead of their direct competitors.

Alignment

The sales team value their time against opportunities to gain commission and so can be difficult to gather in one place. Therefore Dawn ensured that the sessions were all half-day and where possible she scheduled them over lunch. She also made the interventions highly applicable by discussing specific example of sales that had been carried out recently. The external facilitator ensured that these sessions ran smoothly with the minimum amount of conflict. They also included the CEO in one session to demonstrate organizational commitment.

Measurement

Dawn incorporated a number of metrics into her evaluation:

- *Profitability of complex sales* as a running measure in the six months prior to training, the 12 months of the intervention and the following six months. This initial measure was based on the avoidance of liquidated damages for installation. This demonstrated an average 4.5 per cent increase in the profitability of the sales, with a reduction of 12.5 per cent in unprofitable or onerous sales. Ongoing evaluation of the profitability of sales will be assessed over the lifetime of the project, typically running in numbers of years.

- *Skill levels of individual salespeople* as measured through performance management.

- *Receptivity of sales managers* to the intervention and qualitative feedback they provided. In particular, they had realized that some of the salespeople were overly protective of their clients, ensuring that they were the only ones able to service that client through protecting important details. This meant that a team view was less effective and also that the service to the client was less effective. Therefore, the head of sales renewed a central database of client details, with a great deal more information. He also made a further adaptation to the commission structure to include a team-based element where every member would benefit from each sale made by the team as a whole.

- *Key performance indicators (KPIs)* were rewritten to incorporate a profit-based approach to the sales which reinforced the need to build long-term mutually beneficial relationships with clients.

- *Customer satisfaction* – the head of sales conducted six-monthly customer review meetings at which he gathered feedback on their satisfaction with the service that they received. The customers were not informed of the change of approach, but were generally pleased that the glitches that they had experienced before, usually caused by undersold products, were less and less evident.

The utility of this intervention was strong. Utility = perceived value/cost.

The perceived value both to the business, sales team and individual salespeople was high.

The cost to the business was primarily in time as well as the cost of the individual facilitator ($1,750 per day for a total of seven days)

Therefore the utility of this intervention was high. Dawn communicated its success across the organizational intranet and also used a PR agency to place an article in the professional sales and HR journals.

DIAGNOSTIC QUESTIONNAIRE

1 *Subject of evaluation:*
   - What is the learning that you are evaluating?
   - What forms of evaluations are available (eg ROI, skills improvement in the workplace, customer satisfaction, etc)?

2 *Consumers of evaluation:*
   - Who are the stakeholders that should be consulted?
   - What are their expectations of what the learning will provide?
     - Are these realistic expectations?
     - If not, how will you manage their expectations?
   - How do the needs and wants of stakeholders vary?
     - Who are the most important stakeholders and how can you privilege their expectations?
   - Is there a theme of expectations against which you can design your evaluation?

3 *Design of evaluation*
   Which of the models is most appropriate to your specific learning and development? These questions aim to identify the form of evaluation that is most appropriate to your situation. You may find it useful to apply at least two forms of evaluation as each offers a slightly different perspective on the value of the intervention.
   - Benchmarking:
     - Do you want the evaluation to show how you compare with competitors and others in your industry?
     - Do you want to understand how others have honed their learning to get more out of it? Or to avoid issues?
   - Kirkpatrick's level of evaluation:
     - Do you want to assess every part of the delivery of learning? Particularly useful where a response to immediate training is important.
   - CIRO:
     - Are you able to integrate evaluation at every stage of the intervention?
     - Can you integrate it with business needs as well as individual and content (eg knowledge, skill, attitude, behaviour)?

- Is the content of learning measurable enough for this to be an effective approach?
- RAM:
  - Can you take a more holistic and business-focused approach?
  - Are you able to clearly identify the business drivers and address them through learning and development?
  - Can you embed evaluation at every point of the intervention to ensure it is aligned with business needs?
- Collaborative evaluation:
  - Is this a standard learning that others in your industry may also undertake?
  - Have the providers carried out an evaluation of their own? (If so be extra vigilant as they may present the data in the best light.)
- Individual evaluation:
  - Is the learning highly individualized? In which case the lead for it should come from the individual learner themself.

4 *Information available*
  - What information do you need to gather?
    - What information is easily accessible?
    - Which of the information is particularly valuable?
    - Is there some easily gathered information that demonstrates success which you can easily share to build support for your programme?

5 *Review of evaluation*
  - Once you have completed the evaluation, review its effectiveness:
    - How effective was your evaluation in identifying specifically the elements of your programme that were both most and least effective?
    - What would you change for the next evaluation?
    - Whom would you work with? Are there teams whose input you did not really need? Were there teams you missed out and wished you hadn't?

Conclusion

08

Introduction

This book provides an initial introduction to learning and development in the workplace. It has given you some of the theoretical background as well as practical pointers to managing a learning and development function. However, it is very much an introduction. Ideally, you will be able to read it along with colleagues who share your interest and can support you in delivering high-quality interventions. You may also find it useful to join with colleagues from your local CIPD to pick up tips and pointers, or perhaps even share resources.

We have considered learning and development as a key tool to gain and retain competitive advantage for your organization. Some would say that this treats employees like tools and indeed it is a perennial difficulty that once 'developed', employees may well choose to move on to bigger and better things. That is why learning and development must be embedded in the organization as part of a coherent and aligned HR strategy that builds engagement among employees. Where this is done, then the rewards of learning and development are more likely to be reaped.

Ongoing approaches and trends for learning and development

The 2013 learning and development survey from the CIPD asked respondents to choose their top three from a list of 14 major organizational changes that would impact learning and development in the next few years. Their top areas for change were:

1 greater integration of coaching, organizational development and performance management to drive organizational change;

2 greater responsibility devolved to learners and line managers;

3 more emphasis on monitoring, measuring and evaluating training effectiveness.

Even more interesting, the five least important organizational changes were:

1 more use of apps designed for smartphones and other mobile devices;

2 more use of collaborative and social learning;

3 greater centralization of learning and talent development as a function;

4 less use of classroom and trainer-led instruction;

5 more use of social networking (eg Twitter, Facebook, LinkedIn, Yammer, Jive).

There may be a failure of imagination here, but it seems to me that the adage 'same old, same old' applies. Learning and development professionals are facing the same challenges and issues in supporting learning and ensuring that it meets long-term organizational requirements. Learning and development is about enabling individuals and groups to enhance their capabilities – supporting them in accessing learning. It is good to be reminded of this – in the hurly-burly of trying to provide the best outcome for learners and the organization, buffeted by consultancy offers and technology's latest fads, it is easy to forget the main thing. This survey reminds us – it is about learners learning and organizations building capability. Let's hope we are not distracted from this essential and very worthwhile task.

Breaking tools and techniques for learning and development

The major shift has been one in attitude. Employees are now expected to shift to lifelong learning instead of discrete interventions that bring them up to the knowledge or skill level required. This requires the learning and development function to provide an ongoing 'stretch' for employees at all levels. This needs to be demand-led, with a focus on provision of learning opportunities rather than specific interventions. This cultural leap is equivalent to that of the move from training in classrooms to learning and development. It requires employees to be highly self-aware and self-directed in accessing learning opportunities. This will often be those situations that they encounter on the job and then learn from in the ways described by Schön (1983), and discussed in Chapter 6. This is also an ideal way of embedding social learning and encouraging employees to manage their learning through a 'living e-technology', which they themselves can adapt and write. This all requires careful facilitation and focus by the learning and development practitioner, with a keen eye as to what will serve the organizational interests best.

The neurology of learning indicates that our brains are highly 'plastic'. That is they are constantly growing and changing to adapt to the challenges we currently face. Constant and ongoing self-directed development is a strong vehicle for harnessing the plasticity of the brain.

Gaming is a further area of interest for learning and development. Games are played by most people and are an excellent example of learning. Consider FIFA 14 – a popular football simulation video game. It involves complex social rules, requiring collaboration and mutual support to reach a winning strategy, which must be persevered with for hours. Management simulations are an early example of this – with the use of technology, highly complex games can be designed for developing both skills and knowledge in employees.

From steady state to ready state

In 2012 the CIPD conducted research into potential futures for learning and development. Their conclusions were:

- In a bid to be organized, the discipline of a systematic approach can become stale and can inhibit innovation and creativity in our interventions. It is good sometimes to reconsider what we are trying to achieve and almost 'start afresh'.
- Cognitive psychology offers many avenues to support learning, including:
  - how to understand and harness the flexible and plastic brain;
  - how to work with heuristics and biases;
  - how to support employees in getting into 'flow' – when work is truly enjoyable;
  - how to develop learning for all age groups, particularly as the retirement age is put further and further back;
  - addressing the challenge of 'smart drugs' or cognitive enhancers.

This research report suggests new avenues for learning and development and provides interesting reading. It can be accessed from the CIPD website (**www.cipd.co.uk**).

Individual cases

From time to time exceptional individuals emerge. They may not be recognized by their current management team or alternatively they may be recognized as having full potential. These individuals, in my experience, often do not recognize their own capability and need to be encouraged and developed. As L&D professionals we frequently work within processes and procedures that may blind us to recognizing these individuals. It is worth, every so often, checking to see if an exceptional employee has turned up. They may be recognized by outstanding performance on an ability test or selection tasks. They are likely to be highly tenacious and also have a strong emotional intelligence. They may well actively seek to hide their own capability. However, if you are able to develop them they may provide a clear competitive advantage for your organization and it is worth putting in extra resources in order to develop their capabilities.

There is also a case to be made for providing more attentive learning and development opportunities to support diversity. The business benefits of diversity are well known. However, successful diversity is difficult to achieve and maintain and the learning and development function has a clear role to play here. For example, it may be appropriate to engage a consultancy to run diversity workshops, run focus groups discussing diversity issues with employee groups, or coach individuals who experience additional challenges, through disability or gender imbalance or being unlike the majority in some other way. It may also involve a package of secondments, or job rotation and mentoring to provide the necessary support to ensure integration and good levels of teamwork.

Final thoughts

As an L&D practitioner you are in a dynamic industry where labels change regularly as you try to demonstrate your value to senior managers. You may find yourself in a role with the title HR business partner – L&D, or HRD consultant or organizational development (OD) manager or people development vice president (VP), to name a few. The key is to focus on the core of each of these types of role: organizational growth through people development. The title used is more likely to reflect the sector than what you will be asked to do.

Interestingly, you may find that you are actually doing many of the same things as you were in the previous organization with a very different title. However, the culture of the organization is likely to differ in ways that are both obvious and also subtle. It is easy to become complacent once the primary differences have been identified and to miss the importance of some of the more subtle cues. This is particularly important in HR and L&D where the ambiguous hints are an essential indication of the potential new direction of the organization as well as the new interventions that will be needed to support the changed organization.

As you develop your own capability in this area remember:

- Keep up to date with what is going on both in your industry as well as in L&D:
  - Use any number of sources to find out the emerging trends.
  - Google new topics.
  - Keep up with professional bodies.
  - Keep links with colleagues.
  - Read around your subject.
  - Attend conferences.
  - Make sure your interventions are personalized, compelling and engaging.
  - Don't think about just the training course but about everything that comes with it – the stakeholder communication; by achieving a more consistent set of holistic messages around the training you can ensure better 'stickability' and transfer of the training.
  - In all cases when all of the research is done – trust your judgement.
  - Focus on the business impact of any intervention you may want to introduce.

REFERENCES

Alexander, G and Renshaw, B (2005) *Supercoaching: The missing ingredient for high performance*, Random House Books, London

American Society for Training and Development (ASTD) 1997

Argyris, C and Schön, D A (1974) *Theory in Practice: Increasing professional effectiveness*, Jossey-Bass, San Francisco

Bandura, A (1977) Self-efficacy: Toward a unifying theory of behavioural change, *Psychological Review*, **84** (2), pp 191–215

Bassi, L J, Ludwig, J, McMurrer, D P and VanBuren, M (2000) *Profiting From Learning: Do firms' investments in education and training pay off?* ASTD and Saba, Virginia

Bennett, B, Cunningham, I and Dawes, G (2000) *Self Managed Learning in Action: Putting SML into practice*, Gower Publishing Ltd, Aldershot

Blanchard, K (2007) *Leading at a Higher Level*, p 4 Prentice Hall, New Jersey

Bonk, C J and Graham, C R (eds) (2012) *Handbook of Blended Learning: Global perspectives, local designs*, Pfeiffer Publishing, San Francisco

Burke, E (1790) *Reflections on the Revolution in France*, Oxford World's Classics, Oxford

Chartered Institute of Personnel and Development (2012) *From Steady State to Ready State: A need for fresh thinking in learning and talent development*, CIPD, London

CIPD (2010) survey Learning and talent development Survey covering mainland China, Taiwan and HK

Coca Cola [accessed 27 August 2013] Coca Cola Mission, Vision and Values statements [online] http://www.coca-colacompany.com/our-company/mission-vision-values

Cockman, P, Evans, B and Reynolds, P (1992) *Client-Centred Consulting – A practical guide for internal advisers and trainers*, McGraw-Hill, London

Combs, J, Yongmei, L, Hall, A and Ketchen, D (2006) How much do high performance work practices matter? A meta-analysis of their effects on organizational performance, *Personnel Psychology*, **59**, pp 501–28

Cunningham, I (1999) *The Wisdom of Strategic Learning: The self managed learning solution*, 2nd edn, Gower Publishing Ltd, Aldershot

Dalton, K (2011) *Leadership and Management Development: Developing tomorrow's managers*, Financial Times-Prentice Hall, Harlow

Dotlich, D, Cairo, P and Rhinesmith, S (2006) *Head, Heart, and Guts: How the world's best companies develop complete leaders*, Wiley, San Francisco

Dweck, C (2006) *Mindset: The new psychology of success*, Random House, London

Easterby-Smith, M (1986) *Evaluation of Management Education, Training and Development*, Gower Publishing Ltd, Aldershot

Fahey, L and Narayanan, V K (1986) *Macroenvironmental Analysis for Strategic Management*, West Publishing, St Paul, Minnesota

Handy, Charles B (1976) *Understanding Organizations*, Oxford University Press

Hoeckel, K (2010) Learning for Jobs, OECD *Review of Vocational and Educational Training*, Austria

Hofstede, J G (1984) *Culture's Consequences: International differences in work-related values*, 2nd edn, Beverly Hills, CA

Hofstede (2009) Research in cultures: how to use it in training, in *European J Cross-Cultural Competence and Management* 1 (1), [online] http://www.geerthofstede.com/media/1230/research%20on%20cultures%20 how%20to%20use%20it%20gjh%202009.pdf

Honey, P and Mumford, A (1982) *Manual of Learning Styles*, P Honey, London

Howe, M J A (1980) *The Psychology of Human Learning*, p 2 Harper & Row, New York

Huque, A S and Vyas, L (2008) Expectations and performance: assessment of public service training in Hong Kong, *The International Journal of Human Resource Management*, **19** (1), pp 188–204

Isenhour, L C, Stone, D L and Lien, D (2012) Advancing theory and research on employee behaviour in China, *Journal of Managerial Psychology*, **27** (1), pp 4–8

Jackson, C J, Hobman, E, Jimmieson, N and Martin, R (2008) Comparing different approach and avoidance models of learning and personality in the prediction of work, university and leadership outcomes, *British Journal of Psychology*, 1–30

James, W (1890) *Principles of Psychology*, New York, Holt

Johnson, G, Scholes, K and Whittingdon, R (2008) *Exploring Corporate Strategy*, Harlow, Pearson Education

Kaplan, R S and Norton, D P (1996) *The Balanced Scorecard: Translating strategy into action*, Harvard Business Press Books, Harvard

Kanigel, Robert (1997) *The One Best Way: Frederick Winslow Taylor and the enigma of efficiency*, Penguin-Viking, New York

Kirkpatrick, J and Kirkpatrick, W (2009) The Kirkpatrick model, past, present and future, *Chief Learning Officer*, November, pp 20–23

Kuczera, M and Field, S (2010) Learning for Jobs, OECD *Review of Vocational and Educational Training*, Options for China

Lee, M (2001) A refusal to define HRD, *Human Resource Development International*, **4** (3), pp 327–41

Locke, E A and Latham, G P (1990) *A Theory of Goal Setting and Task Performance*, Prentice-Hall, Englewood Cliffs, N J

Mintzberg, H (1994) *The Rise and Fall of Strategic Planning*, Prentice Hall, New York

Pedler, M, Boydell, T and Burgoyne, J (1991) *The Learning Company: A strategy for sustainable development*, McGraw-Hill, London

Porter, M E (1979) The structure within industries and companies, *Review of Economics and Statistics*, **61**, pp 214–29

Preskill, H, Torres, R T and Martinez-Papponi, B (1999) *Assessing an organization's readiness for learning from evaluative inquiry*, Paper presented at the American Evaluation Association annual conference, Orlando, FL

Purcell, J (2003) Understanding the People and Performance Link: Unlocking the black box research report, Chartered Institute of Personnel and Development

Rotter, J B (1954) *Social learning and clinical psychology*, Prentice Hall, New York

Schön, D (1983) *The Reflective Practitioner: How professionals think in action*, Basic Books inc, USA

Senge, P (2006) *The Fifth Discipline: The art and practice of the learning organization*, 2nd ed, Random House, London

Smith, P J and Sadler-Smith, E (2006) *Learning in Organizations: Complexities and diversities*, Routledge, Oxon

Tilastokeskus (2003) [online] http://www.stat.fi/til/atoi/index.html

Toffler, A (1970) *Future Shock*, Bantam Books/Random House, New York

Toffler, A (1994) Alvin Toffler: Still shocking after all these years, *New Scientist*, 19 March, pp 22–25

Ulrich, D (2005) *HR Value Proposition*, Harvard Business School Press, Boston

Vygotsky, L S (1980) *Mind in Society: The development of higher psychological processes*, President and Fellows of Harvard College

Warr, P, Bird, M and Rackham, N (1970) *Evaluation of Management Training: A practical framework with cases, for evaluating training needs and results*, Gower Press

Winstanley, D (1995) When the pieces don't fit: A stakeholder power matrix to analyse public sector restructuring, *Public Money and Management*, April–June, pp 19–26

The Wolf Report – Review of vocational education (2011) UK Department for Education

Yapp, M (2005) High-potential talent assessment in Grant, P (ed) *Business Psychology in Practice*, Whurr Publishers Ltd, London

Zuckerman, M (2007) *Sensation Seeking and Risky Behavior*, Washington DC, American Psychological Association

INDEX

NB page numbers in *italics* denote material within a table or figure.

EMPLOYEE RELATIONS

Elizabeth Aylott

March 2014
9780749469764
224 pages

REWARD MANAGEMENT

Michael Rose

April 2014
9780749469801
224 pages

EMPLOYMENT LAW

Elizabeth Aylott

May 2014
9780749469740
272 pages

LEARNING & DEVELOPMENT

Rebecca Page-Tickell

June 2014
9780749469887
272 pages

PERFORMANCE MANAGEMENT

Linda Ashdown

July 2014
9780749469979
272 pages

HOW TO CREATE A COACHING CULTURE

Gillian Jones
Ro Gorell

August 2014
9780749469795
272pages

EMPLOYEE ENGAGEMENT

Ted Johns

November 2014
9780749472016
272 pages

The **HR Fundamentals** series offers practical advice to HR professionals starting out in their career, completing CPD training or studying for their professional qualifications with CIPD. The series tackles the core knowledge every HR practitioner needs to develop their career.

All titles:
£29.99
Paperback
234 x 156mm

Also available from Kogan Page

Find out more; visit www.koganpage.com and
sign up for offers and regular e-newsletters.